This book is dedicated to Stephen Lamb, co-director of
Sportsline Media Limited, who has contributed enormously
to the compilation of this book. Also to Les Lenham, who first
got me involved in coaching and who is still a major
influence on my coaching.

And it is dedicated to my son, Tim Dellor, to whom
I obviously conveyed any coaching ability I might have because he
is now adding considerably to my knowledge of cricket. However,
his impressive coaching credentials have not prevented him from
being vulnerable to the ball swinging away outside
off-stump, especially when bowled by his father.

Contents

Cricket

STEPS TO SUCCESS

Please return on or before the last date stamped below.
Contact: 01603 773 114
or 01603 773 224

HUMAN KINETICS

243 765

Library of Congress Cataloging-in-Publication Data

Dellor, Ralph, 1948-
 Cricket / Ralph Dellor.
    p. cm. -- (Steps to success sports series)
 ISBN-13: 978-0-7360-7873-3 (soft cover)
 ISBN-10: 0-7360-7873-8 (soft cover)
 1. Cricket. I. Title.
 GV917.D64 2010
 796.358--dc22

                                    2009037253

ISBN-10: 0-7360-7873-8 (print)
ISBN-13: 978-0-7360-7873-3 (print)

The Web addresses cited in this text were current as of December 2009, unless otherwise noted.

Acquisitions Editor: John Dickinson; **Developmental Editor:** Cynthia McEntire; **Assistant Editor:** Scott Hawkins; **Copyeditor:** Ann Prisland; **Graphic Designer:** Nancy Rasmus; **Graphic Artist:** Julie L. Denzer; **Cover Designer:** Keith Blomberg; **Photographer (cover):** Hamish Blair/Getty Images Sport; **Photographer (interior):** Nigel Farrow; **Photo Manager:** Neil Bernstein; **Visual Production Assistant:** Joyce Brumfield; **Photo Production Manager:** Jason Allen; **Art Manager:** Kelly Hendren; **Associate Art Manager:** Alan L. Wilborn; **Printer:** United Graphics

We thank Shiplake College at Henley-on-Thames for assistance in providing the location for the photo shoot for this book.

Human Kinetics books are available at special discounts for bulk purchase. Special editions or book excerpts can also be created to specification. For details, contact the Special Sales Manager at Human Kinetics.

Printed in the United States of America   10 9 8 7 6 5 4 3 2 1

The paper in this book is certified under a sustainable forestry program.

Human Kinetics
Web site: www.HumanKinetics.com

United States: Human Kinetics
P.O. Box 5076
Champaign, IL 61825-5076
800-747-4457
e-mail: humank@hkusa.com

Canada: Human Kinetics
475 Devonshire Road Unit 100
Windsor, ON N8Y 2L5
800-465-7301 (in Canada only)
e-mail: info@hkcanada.com

Europe: Human Kinetics
107 Bradford Road
Stanningley
Leeds LS28 6AT, United Kingdom
+44 (0) 113 255 5665
e-mail: hk@hkeurope.com

Australia: Human Kinetics
57A Price Avenue
Lower Mitcham, South Australia 5062
08 8372 0999
e-mail: info@hkaustralia.com

New Zealand: Human Kinetics
P.O. Box 80
Torrens Park, South Australia 5062
0800 222 062
e-mail: info@hknewzealand.com

E4660

Climbing the Steps to Cricket Success

For beginning and intermediate players, as well as their teachers and coaches, using the information and practising the skills outlined in *Cricket: Steps to Success* can help build a foundation or add to what players have already accomplished in the sport.

The steps to success are logically arranged to deal with each discipline in cricket. By following the steps, you should improve in all aspects of the game and be more likely to find your niche. That is the great thing about cricket: it accommodates people of all shapes and sizes, and it has a place for everyone. Not all players are skilled in all disciplines. This means that unlike in some other sports, you do not have to master one step before moving on to the next. For example, you do not have to excel at defensive batting (step 5) before moving on to attacking batting (step 6); however, unless you can defend your wicket, you will not be around long enough to play those attacking strokes. Similarly, if you are going to specialise in spin bowling (step 3), you will not want to spend much time on fast bowling (step 2). But regardless of your interest, you will want to have spent time on basic bowling (step 1), which is the foundation for all styles of bowling.

The explanations and accompanying photographs not only provide clear instructions for executing every technique that forms the basis of the game, but they also offer options. You will not be forced to comply with a standard way of playing; rather, you will have the freedom to find what suits you. Experiment to find a style that fits your playing level, your body and your attitude.

Intermediate players already know the basics of the game and the skills required for playing it. *Cricket: Steps to Success* offers more thorough explanations of the necessary techniques than do basic instruction books. Refine and polish your skills with game-specific drills as you move towards playing at an advanced level. Gain more insight into what strokes are appropriate to be played for specific deliveries, which balls you might want to bowl and why, and how you need to think through a match, whether you are a batsman, bowler or wicket-keeper.

If you are a teacher or coach, *Cricket: Steps to Success* provides an easy-to-follow instructional package. If you already have an established teaching system, you can select information, drills, activities and methods of grading that fit your programme. The background section includes a brief history of cricket, information about the type of equipment required, warm-up and cool-down guidelines, ways to avoid injuries and Web-based cricket resources. The book also includes skills, strategies, self-paced drills and methods of evaluating students, plus an extensive cricket glossary. In short, this book is designed for coaches, parents working with their children and players themselves. If you are a player, using this book is like having a coach with you at all times. When you have a problem, you can delve into the book to solve it. One of the great things about cricket is that the player who is honest with himself and admits errors will make more progress and improve. It is important to learn what is wrong and work to eradicate the problem. There is nothing wrong with failing, providing you learn from that failure.

Cricket coaches, even those who were successful players, do not automatically acquire a complete understanding of the mechanics of the game, which is why great players do not always make great, or even adequate, coaches. As a coach, you add pieces of information to your personal database step by step and year by year. *Cricket: Steps to Success* can accelerate that learning process.

Cricket: Steps to Success provides a systematic approach to playing and teaching cricket. Follow this sequence as you work your way through each step:

1. Read the explanation of what is covered in the step, why the step is important, and how to execute or perform the step.

2. Follow the photos and illustrations.

3. Review the missteps, which note common errors and their corrections.

4. Perform the drills. Drills help improve skills through repetition and purposeful practice. Read the directions and record your score. Drills appear near the skill instructions so you can refer to the instructions easily if you have trouble with the drill.

As coaches and cricketers, you can help yourselves considerably if you keep one thought at the forefront of your mind: cricket is really a simple game. It might not appear so when you first encounter it, but it is the players themselves (often aided and abetted by their coaches!) who make it complicated. Remember, the best players are those who do the simple things better than anybody else. Watch the great players and see how they go about their game. Compare the strokes they play and their bowling actions with the examples that appear in this book to see just how close you are to them. Of course, the best players perform well consistently; because they apply the basics, they can attain the necessary consistency to perform well at the top level.

Throughout this book, I refer to the male sex. This is merely for ease of writing and is in no way intended to ignore females. Women's cricket is growing rapidly, and the standard of play is improving dramatically. Cricket is most definitely a sport for both sexes, and what girls might lack in terms of physical strength, they compensate for by having excellent techniques. I also refer to the right-handed player as the norm, again for stylistic purposes. Unless left-handed players are specifically mentioned, the same technique applies, but in a mirror image.

Make *Cricket: Steps to Success* work for you. Learn the game from scratch as a beginner, sharpen your skills as an intermediate player, teach the game using a systematic approach or coach with a more comprehensive understanding of the game. Even if you are an advanced player, you will find drills that challenge your skills and strategy tips that might give you an edge over opponents.

The reward for completing the steps to success is whatever you want it to be. For some, playing cricket is just plain fun. For those of you who enjoy competition, a world of league cricket is out there, waiting to test your skills at whatever level you attain. Enjoy this step-by-step journey to developing cricket skills, building confidence and experiencing progress. Whether you are male or female, right- or left-handed, go out and enjoy your cricket. *Cricket: Steps to Success* is ready to take you several steps closer to becoming the best player you can be. The objective, whether you are starting out as a cricketer or are already experienced, is to make you a more successful player. The more successful you are, the more you will enjoy the game. Have fun!

The Sport of Cricket

White balls, black sightscreens, coloured clothing, TV referrals, fourth umpires, blaring music—what on earth would W.G. Grace have made of it all? Undoubtedly, the game developed greatly in the days of cricket's grand old man (not least due to his influence), but it is hard to imagine a period of more rapid evolution than the past 30 years. The advent of the Indian Premier League as the game's modern financial powerhouse contrasts starkly with cricket's humble origins in England centuries ago.

So how did it all begin? Ancient references abound to bat and ball games in England and Europe, and it has even been suggested that China was cricket's cradle. But it is more widely acknowledged that the modern game originated in England and was played by shepherds, whose sheep would have kept the grass short enough to permit the procedure of rolling the ball along the ground. A shepherd's crook might well have been the prototype bat, given the curved shape of the earliest known specimens. A ball could have been made of matted wool, held together by wax. And what better target for the bowler than a wicket gate from a sheep's pen?

Gradually, the ball developed a broadly uniform shape. Stuffing became the means of forming the centre, with a covering of leather stitched around it. Regulations followed concerning ball weight and then size. Meanwhile, the stick was honed into a club, initially with a distinctive curve at the bottom, designed to deal with underarm deliveries bowled along the ground. Over time, a shoulder to the bat emerged, followed by the splice that made it look much as it does now.

The wardrobe accounts of Edward I in 1300 contain one of the earliest references to cricket. It concerns payment to the chaplain of the King's son "for monies paid out himself or by the hands of others, for the said Prince playing at creag and other sports at Westminster on 10th March." A more precise reference occurs in 1598, when a witness at a court case on disputed land mentions that "he and diverse of his fellows did runne and play there at creckett and other plaies."

Much evidence follows of cricket incurring the wrath of the Church. In Sussex, a case was brought against six men for playing cricket instead of attending Sunday evensong, and two churchwardens were admonished for joining them. In 1629 a curate, Henry Cuffin, was castigated for "playing at crickets" on the Sabbath "in a very unseemly fashion with boys and other very mean and base persons."

The growing importance of wagers on matches was highlighted in a court case in 1646 over the non-payment of a cricket-related bet, and by the end of the century there was a press report of an 11-a-side match in Sussex played for "fifty guineas apiece." By the 1700s, private clubs were flourishing, and cricket, by then acknowledged as a conventional sport, represented a comparatively new opportunity for gambling.

Evidence of a recognised form of the game existed in 1706, and although the Laws were not formulated until nearly 40 years later, the earlier document shows how the various local versions of cricket had come together in an accepted form. The ball was made of leather and bowled at one of two batsmen who defended a wicket comprising two stumps with a single bail across the top; there were also fielders, umpires and scorers.

A significant part in cricket's development was played by the village of Hambledon in Hampshire, which boasted a team including so many of the leading players of the era between 1772 and 1781 that they won more than half of 51 matches played against All England. The village's legendary ground at Broadhalfpenny Down survives still, as does the Bat and Ball Inn just across the road. In 1775, at the Artillery Ground in London, the last Hambledon batsman made the 14 runs required to beat Kent, despite being "bowled" on no less than three occasions when the ball went between the two stumps without removing the bail. A third stump was added the following year to eradicate this absurdity.

Hambledon eventually left Broadhalfpenny Down for nearby Windmill Down, but such was their status that many of their matches were played in London. As Hambledon's influence declined towards the end of the century, London clubs grew in importance. One such club was Marylebone, which was set up at a new ground opened by Thomas Lord, where Dorset Square is now situated. Marylebone Cricket Club (MCC) was established in 1787, the year the venue opened.

Lord was twice obliged to move his ground, first half a mile northwards, where he replanted the turf at North Bank. The MCC went with him, as it did when the new Regent's Canal was dug through the second ground in 1814. Lord picked up his turf again and took over a horticultural nursery in St. John's Wood. Thus was Lord's Cricket Ground established, where the MCC exists today. By 1788 the club was authoritative enough to declare an overhaul of the Laws, of which it is still the guardian.

In 1828 the MCC was compelled to approve roundarm bowling, which developed from the previous underarm technique in which the bowler's hand was as high as his elbow. Barely had the new Law been introduced than it was broken: Players went further and bowled from shoulder height, forcing the MCC to endorse such bowling as legitimate in 1835. By 1864 overarm bowling was permitted, and the game was well on its way to appearing broadly as it does today.

Crowds of people were now flocking to watch the big matches, heralding cricket's emergence as a major spectator sport. Important matches included Gentlemen versus Players (amateurs against professionals), North versus South, Nottingham versus Sheffield and various games involving the MCC. But before long, the Victorian public had tired of such fare, engaging instead with county cricket and, later still, with Test cricket. In both cases, the public was demonstrating a need for representative rather than commercial forms of the game.

Test cricket is officially regarded as having begun in 1877 when Australia defeated England by 45 runs in Melbourne. The Ashes legend was born five years later, and in 1889 South Africa became the third Test-playing nation. The West Indies entered the international arena in 1928, just two years before New Zealand. In 1932 India joined Test cricket, and 20 years later so did the seventh Test nation, Pakistan. Sri Lanka joined in 1982, followed by Zimbabwe in 1992 and Bangladesh in 2000.

To the purist, Test cricket remains the ultimate form of the game. It is played over five days, allowing the fullest opportunity to display talent. It is a stage W.G. Grace bestrode in its early years, and where generations of cricketing legends have taken their bows, from Donald Bradman, surely the greatest batsmen of them all, through Garfield Sobers, unchallenged in all-round versatility, to Shane Warne, a latter-day spin wizard. It has also produced the game's greatest controversies, never more than in the Bodyline Ashes series of 1932 to 1933, when the fast-bowling tactics of the England captain threatened diplomatic relations between his country and Australia.

There was no clear-cut commencement of the County Championship. County clubs existed from around 1825, and talk of a champion county was initially no more than a bragging right when a team had an outstanding season. In 1864 Surrey were proclaimed champions after winning six and drawing their other two matches. Nine years later, a meeting in London drew up some rules for the foundation of an authentic championship.

Nine counties were involved beginning in 1873. Derbyshire, Gloucestershire, Kent, Lancashire, Middlesex, Nottinghamshire, Surrey, Sussex and Yorkshire took part, using various means for determining the champions. Essex, Hampshire, Leicestershire, Somerset and Warwickshire joined by 1895, the year that marks, for many, the commencement of the established championship. The number increased to 15 four years later when Worcestershire were included, followed by Northamptonshire in 1905. Glamorgan's admittance in 1921 increased the number to 17, where it remained until 1992 when Durham were accorded first-class status.

The birth of one-day internationals, like so much in cricket, owed more than a little to the weather. When England were in Australia in 1970 to 1971, persistent rain forced the abandonment of the third Test in Melbourne. Out of courtesy to the spectators, a limited-overs match was hastily arranged to take place on what would have been the final day of the Test. It was 40 overs a side and proved to be an instant hit, leading to the short, one-day series and the birth of the World Cup less than five years later. Since that unscheduled encounter in 1971, more than 2,500 one-day internationals have been played across the world.

Amongst innumerable one-day competitions, the World Cup remains the most prestigious. The first two tournaments were won by Clive Lloyd's West Indies, who were favourites to take the third but were upset by Kapil Dev's India. England, who have yet to raise the trophy, were finalists but were beaten in 1987, when Australia won, and mauled in 1992 after Imran Khan famously urged his Pakistan team to emulate the action of a cornered tiger. Australia were surprisingly beaten by Sri Lanka four years later but have dominated all three tournaments since.

The venue for the first three World Cups was England, where one-day cricket had been popular since the inauguration of the Gillette Cup in 1963, a move that rescued the county game from potentially terminal decline. Gillette matches were 65 overs a side in the first year, reduced to 60 the following season. They remained as such, under successive sponsors, until their reduction to the one-day international measure of 50 overs in 1999.

The year 1969 saw the start of the Sunday League, the next domestic limited-overs contest. Simplicity was the cornerstone of its success: It started at two o'clock every Sunday and was 40 overs a side, with bowlers allowed run-ups of no more than 15 yards (13.7 m). This restriction was later lifted among other changes, which included allowing the matches to start earlier, and it became a 50-over competition in 1993 before falling back again to 40.

England's third one-day tournament, the Benson & Hedges Cup, was launched in 1972. It started on a league basis, with the country partitioned into qualifying leagues before the knockout phase, with 55 overs available between 1972 and 1995. It then went to 50 overs and was eventually replaced in 2003 by a new competition designed to appeal to a different section of the public. The Twenty20 surfed a wave of hard sell and hype, but whatever the quibblers thought, it has been spectacularly and commercially successful.

As cricket put down roots across the world, often following the empire-building armed forces, England was the role model for other nations. Just as the County Championship evolved, so did domestic cricket elsewhere. The Sheffield Shield was born in Australia, the Currie Cup in South Africa and the Quaid-e-Azam Trophy in Pakistan. As in England, successive sponsors gave their names to the different first-class or one-day tournaments. And however inconsistent England may be in playing one-day cricket, there can be no doubting her continuing influence on its evolution. The Twenty20 format was soon adopted internationally, with India winning World Cup silverware in 2007 and Pakistan in 2009.

FIELD OF PLAY

When you consider the complexities of the strategy that underlie a match, the oft-used expression "cricket is like a game of chess played on grass" makes perfect sense. But what about the board and the pieces—the field of play and the players?

A stylised ground is regarded as being oval in shape. In fact, the oldest ground on which Test cricket is played in England is known as the Oval, located in southeast London. However, not only is the playing surface of the Oval not oval, even though the perimeter wall of the ground is, few other grounds conform to the assumed shape. Irregular sizes and shapes abound to give each ground a character of its own. In New Zealand, for example, most major grounds double as Rugby Union venues, with that sport dominating the structure of the stadia. At the home of the Kent County Cricket Club, the St. Lawrence Ground in Canterbury, there used to be a historic lime tree growing within the boundary itself. When it was finally felled by a storm, what did the authorities do? Did they take the opportunity to eradicate any trace of it? Of course not! They made the quintessentially English decision to plant another in its place.

The Laws of Cricket do not set a distance for the boundary from the stumps, let alone define the shape of the field. However, the national governing bodies and the International Cricket Council lay down minimum sizes for certain competitions. That is one of the joys of cricket: It can accommodate players on the village green as well as in a great arena. There are, however, strict regulations about the size of the pitch and the wicket.

Those two terms—pitch and wicket—have become interchangeable in recent times; to be slightly pedantic, the pitch refers to the strip of carefully prepared grass between the two sets of stumps or the two wickets. So, although a wicket is never referred to as a pitch, a pitch is often called a wicket.

The Laws state that the pitch will be 22 yards (20.1 m) long and 10 feet (3 m) wide (figure 1, page xii). Although it might sound archaic to refer to imperial rather than metric measurements (both are now mentioned in the Laws), consider the fact that the 22-yard measurement came about in the 18th century because it was the length of a standard agricultural chain. To delve further, a chain is a tenth of a furlong that, in turn, is an eighth of a mile (.2 km). It is derived from "furrow-long," or the length of a furrow characteristic of Anglo-Saxon farming. The game is deeply rooted in history.

At either end of the pitch, lines on the ground denote the creases. The bowling crease indicates where the stumps go and from where the bowler must deliver the ball. The popping crease is the area within which the batsman must be to avoid being stumped or run-out. The wicket itself consists of three stumps with two bails across the top (figure 2, page xiii). At least one of these bails must be dislodged for a batsman to be bowled, run-out or stumped.

As for the fielders, they are positioned according to the state of the game, the type of bowler and the strategy being employed by the captain. In general, there are three categories of fielders, each with its own job to do. There are the close catchers—the slips, gully, short legs and those in the appropriately termed silly positions—who are placed specifically to accept any chance of a catch. Captains use fielders in these positions when they are on the attack and taking wickets is of prime importance.

Then there are the single savers. Of course, they also try to stop the fours and will readily accept any catches coming their way if they can. However, their primary function is to prevent the batsmen from taking quick runs or to run them out if they try. These fielders patrol the covers on one side of the pitch, the square leg and mid-wicket area on the other and the mid-on and mid-off.

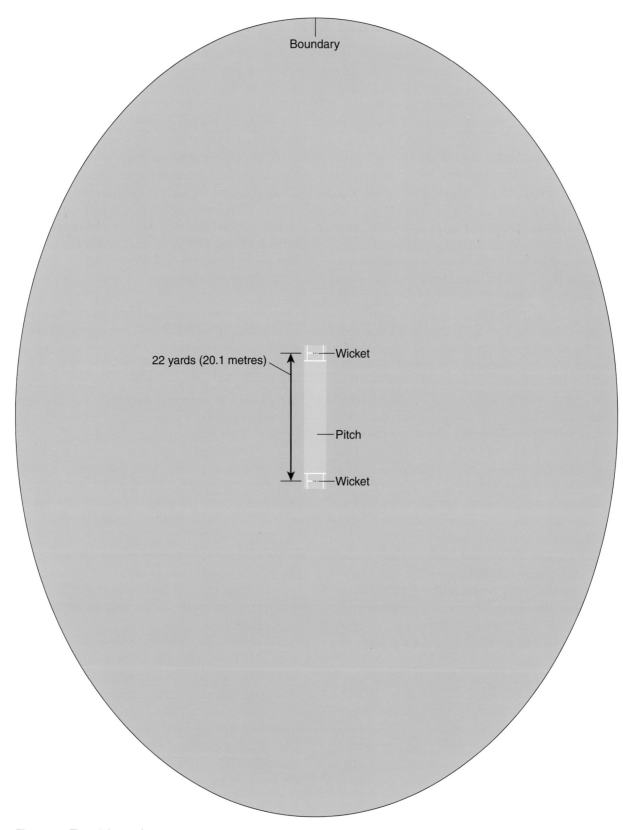

Figure 1 The wicket and creases.

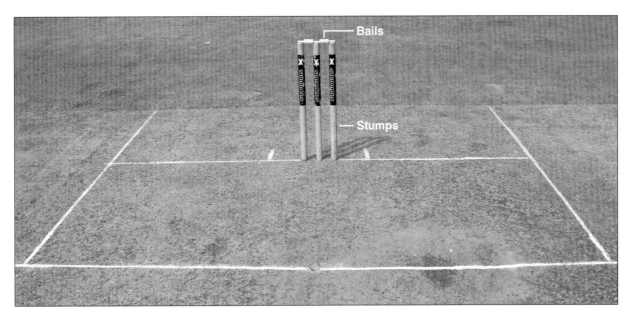

Figure 2 Parts of the wicket.

Further out, on the boundary edge, are the deep fielders. Their job is to stop the ball from crossing the boundary for four. If the ball is struck straight to them, they should be able to cut the scoring potential of a stroke down to a single run. But there is always the possibility of a catch, especially when the batsman is trying to hit the ball over the boundary for six. With deep fielders in the right place and a slight misjudgement from the batsman, another wicket can fall. Whereas a bowler might prefer the satisfaction of seeing a catch off his bowling close to the wicket as a reward for his skill, he will never say no to one that results from a batsman's mistake. Bad balls as well as good ones result in wickets, and there are no pictures in the scorebook to illustrate just how the wickets fell.

Recognised fielding positions have evolved over the course of time, but there is no compulsion to have men posted in the usual positions. Often a game can be turned by some fine adjustment to the field, which is why the captain may be seen moving a fielder just a little one way or the other.

The positions shown in figure 3 (page xiv) are the most commonly used ones and are where the fielders normally stand if they are posted to certain positions. These are only approximations and can vary considerably. However, they are the positions to which the ball is most likely to go for certain types of bowlers, given the knowledge gained from experience. As bowling styles develop and batsmen employ different techniques to counter them, so fielding positions go in and out of fashion.

Even the most unathletic fielder might have a valuable role to play for the team by becoming a specialist close catcher. He might not be very mobile, but he may be adept at taking anything in the air that comes within reach. On the other hand, a superb athlete who is fast across the ground and has a powerful throw is invaluable in the outfield. One of the joys of cricket is that there is room for all types, shapes and sizes. The higher up in the game you go, the greater the need for proficiency in all positions in the field, but there is still a place for everybody.

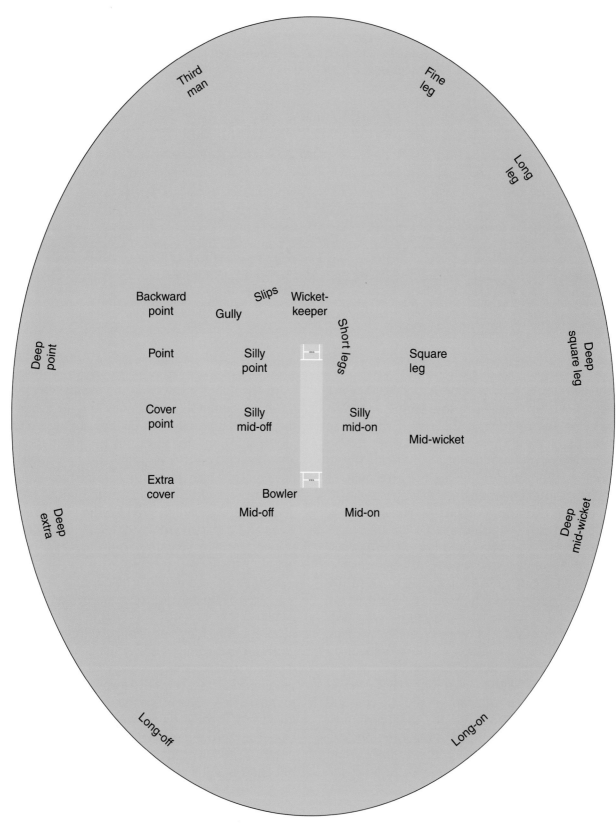

Figure 3 Fielding positions.

PLAYING CRICKET

Cricket is a simple game, yet that is hard for someone to believe who first comes to it and tries to pare away the intricacies in order to get to the basics. There is a famous tea towel on which those basics are made anything but clear to someone who knows nothing about the game. It reads as follows:

> You have two sides, one out in the field and one in. Each man that's in the side that's in goes out, and when he's out he comes in and the next man goes in until he's out. When they are all out, the side that's out comes in and the side that's been in goes out and tries to get those coming in out. Sometimes you get men still in and not out.

When a man goes out to go in, the men who are out try to get him out, and when he is out he goes in and the next man in goes out and goes in. There are two men called umpires who stay all out all the time and they decide when the men who are in are out. When both sides have been in and all the men have been out, and both sides have been out twice after all the men have been in, including those who are not out, that is the end of the game!

Someone who knew nothing about the game before reading that description not only would still know nothing about the game but would probably have given up any intention of finding out what makes this game the best there is.

Like most clever pieces of satirical writing, there is an element of truth in the tea towel text, albeit contorted into a grotesque travesty. But if the contortions are ironed out, it should be possible to gain an understanding of what the game is all about.

There are, indeed, two sides of 11 players each. A coin toss is used to determine which side bats and which fields. Traditionally, the captain of the home side flicks the coin into the air, and the visiting skipper calls heads or tails. The winner of the toss then makes a decision based on the state of the pitch, weather conditions, the composition of the teams or simply intuition whether to bat or field first.

If the captain decides to bat first, two of his side, the opening batsmen, go out to face the bowling. The opposing captain usually picks the fastest bowlers in his team to operate with the new ball. Its hardness causes it to bounce more, and the prominent seam and shine will help it move off a straight line as it travels through the air and when it is pitched. This means that the opening batsmen usually have the best technique and are prepared to face the fast bowling that is likely to come their way.

The objective of the fielding side is to prevent the batsmen from scoring runs and to get them out. The five most common ways to dismiss a batsman are these:

1. **Bowled.** The batsman misses the ball, and it strikes the stumps (the wicket).

2. **Leg before wicket (LBW).** The batsman misses the ball, but the batsman's leg prevents the ball from hitting the wicket. Some qualifications make this Law complex. For example, the ball cannot pitch outside the line of the leg stump, and it must not touch the bat. LBW decisions tend to be contentious.

3. **Caught.** The ball is caught by a member of the fielding side after it hits the bat and before it touches the ground.

4. **Run-out.** When attempting to run, the batsman does not have part of his person or bat grounded behind the popping crease (figure 4, page xvi) at the moment the ball hits the stumps after being thrown by a fielder, or when someone, usually the wicket-keeper, takes the return and removes the bails.

5. **Stumped.** The batsman misses the ball and is out of his ground when the ball reaches the wicket-keeper, who removes the bails.

A batsman also can be out if he handles the ball, is timed out, hits the ball twice, hits the wicket or obstructs the field. These, however, are very rare occurrences.

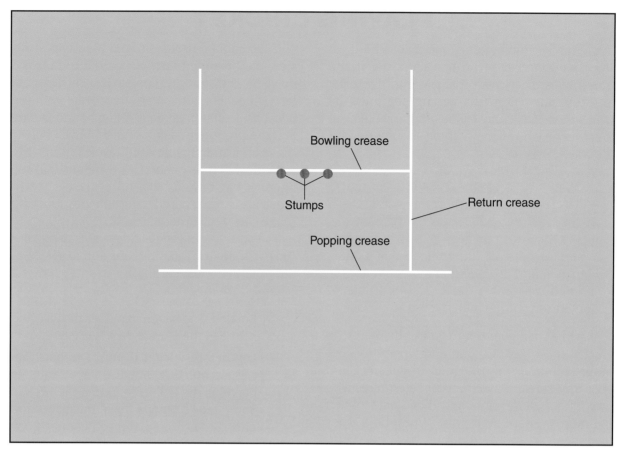

Figure 4   The bowling crease, return creases, and popping crease.

While the batsmen are trying to stop the bowlers from getting them out, they also must score runs. It is often fairly easy for the batsmen simply to concentrate on staying in, but when they try to score runs, they must take more risks. That is the great dilemma of the game. The bowlers know this, too, and strive to prevent the batsmen from scoring runs. The bowlers know that the time will come when the batsmen have to increase the risks they take in order to put runs on the scoreboard.

Runs are scored when a batsman has hit the ball far enough away from a fielder to be able to run to the other end of the pitch before the fielder can return the ball to either set of stumps. For this reason, single runs are the most common, but it is not unusual to run twos or threes. If the ball is hit to the boundary along the ground, the batsman gets four runs without actually having to run. If the ball is hit over the boundary without bouncing in the field of play, six runs are added to the score. However, adding a maximum number of runs requires hitting the ball in the air, which increases the risk of the ball being caught. Attempting to hit the ball that hard increases the risk of missing it completely.

In addition to the runs scored by the batsmen, there are extras. These are additional runs that accrue largely through mistakes by the fielding team and their bowlers. If the bowler transgresses by overstepping the popping crease in the act of bowling, for example, the umpire will call, "No-ball," and one run is added to the total. But the batsman can score runs off that delivery as well, safe in the knowledge that the Laws of Cricket state that he cannot be out off a no-ball unless he is run-out. Similarly, a run is scored if the umpire considers the ball was bowled beyond the reach of the batsman. If a ball goes past the batsman, does not hit the wicket and is not stopped by the wicket-keeper, the batsman can run; this is recorded as a bye. A leg bye is added to the total when the batsmen complete a run after the ball has hit the batsman's body as opposed to his bat.

It is this balance of risk that is at the very heart of the game, for it affects the thinking of the fielding captain as well as the batsmen. The fielding captain knows that he can position fielders in such a way that they might well stop runs from being scored, but by being in those positions, they may not be ideally placed to take catches and hasten the demise of the batting side. Furthermore, bowlers get tired. The captain has to decide whether he can risk one more over from his opening bowler, who has perhaps taken three wickets and is bowling well, or rest him in the hope that he will come back into the attack later, refreshed and ready to strike again.

These are the tactical conundrums that make cricket the game it is. The strategic battle that unfolds is almost as important to the developing drama of a match as the technical contest between bat and ball. The higher up in the game's levels you go, the more important the captain's role is in achieving the desired outcome, as will be seen in Step 9, where the roles of the captain and other members of the team are examined in more detail. At lower levels, the captain's influence is limited by the technique of the players at his disposal; at the very top, where there is a high level of technical competence among players, it is the inspired bowling change or subtle alteration in the position of a fielder that can make the vital difference between winning and losing. And winning is the object of the game: If you are not playing to win, do not bother to keep score.

The scorers have a long and distinguished place in the game as the accountants of cricket. At one time they were known as the notchers, literally cutting notches in a piece of wood as runs were scored. The task has developed, like the game itself, so that now scorers in the top echelons of the game rely on computers with sophisticated software programmes. But they are the bookkeepers, subservient to the two umpires who are out in the middle making the vital decisions relating to the Laws.

Remember the tea towel: "There are two men called umpires who stay all out all the time and they decide when the men who are in are out." In essence this is exactly what they do, adjudicating on appeals for wickets. The batsman is hit on the pad, the bowler appeals with a raucous cry of "How's that?" and the umpire decides whether the ball meets all the criteria for an LBW decision. If the umpire is happy that it does, he raises his index finger to signify that the batsman is out. The umpires adjudicate on all matters, from counting the six legitimate balls in an over to deciding if conditions are fit for play, generally ensuring that the Laws of Cricket are adhered to in all their minutiae. And the umpires are out there for the whole game. Umpires never win the toss and sit in the comfort of the pavilion watching their team-mates bat!

So, when the bowlers have taken their wickets, the batsmen have scored their runs, the umpires have given their decisions and the scorers have recorded the progress of the game, we reach a result. Put simply, the side that scores the more runs wins. However, this is cricket, and it is not always as straightforward as that. In a limited-overs game, the rule generally holds. Side A bat for the full quota of 50 overs and score, say, 260 for the loss of five wickets. Side B reach 240 for eight in 50 overs, and so side A win by 20 runs. Or, if side B had scored 261 for eight in 49.5 overs, side B would have won by two wickets. If the scores had finished level after both sides had faced the same number of overs, then the result would have been a tie, irrespective of the number of wickets lost.

In matches where time is allotted for the completion of the match, be it two innings a side or one, another result becomes possible—a draw—and another means of achieving a result enters the equation. This is called a declaration. If the captain of the side batting first considers there are enough runs on the board and that the other side can be bowled out in the time available, he will declare the innings closed. For example, side A reach 200 for five with two and a half hours of playing time remaining. The captain declares in the belief that side B can be bowled out in the time available before scoring 201 runs. Side B are bowled out for 160, and side A win by 40 runs. Or side B score 201 for seven and win by three wickets. If side B finish on only 90 for nine, the match is drawn, as it is if side B score 200 for nine; if they score 200 all out, it is a tie.

The shorter versions of the game—Twenty20 or other limited-overs matches during which a team's innings are restricted in overs rather than time—can generate instant excitement, but they cannot match a two-innings game that gives the ebb and flow of superiority time to unfold. In the shorter matches, it is the clock that dictates the pattern of play, rather than a figure on the scoreboard that indicates how long there is to go. There is nothing to equal the drama and tension of a five-day Test match that reaches the last available over with any of the four results still possible. That is cricket at its very best.

WARM-UP AND COOL-DOWN

Gone are the days when players fell out of the pub and went straight out onto the field to play. More thought is given to the game and how it is played, so it is not enough to just go out and face or bowl the first ball. That statement in itself encapsulates one of the problems associated with preparing to play cricket. An all-day game might start at 11:00 a.m. The players might well arrive at the ground ready to begin their pre-performance routines at 10:00 a.m. They all go through the team warm-up and then some fielding practice before undertaking routines specific to their roles in the game. The opening bowler is fired up and ready to go, except that his captain wins the toss and decides to bat first. It might be mid-afternoon before that bowler is called into action, and by then he has been sitting around and has had lunch.

For each session of play, it is important to prepare properly, not only physically but mentally. Cricket is a cerebral game, with so many elements played in the mind. It is also a team game, so the first preparation activity should be a team warm-up.

Some doubt has been cast on the physical value of a static warm-up routine. In fact, the doctor in charge of a British Olympic team once opined that human muscles and tendons have evolved to react immediately. Early man would have needed his body to be ready for action, without the benefit of a warm-up, if he had to run away from a wild animal. Be that as it may, most medical opinion is that the body will work more efficiently and will be less prone to injury if it is properly warmed up before serious sporting activity.

For a team to arrive at the venue and then go through a warm-up routine as a unit is also a good way to prepare mentally. The team ethic is instilled, and all extraneous thoughts and concerns brought along to the match can be forgotten. This is the time to focus on enjoying cricket and to get away from personal, school or professional problems.

Before doing any stretching exercises, be they dynamic or static, make sure to raise each player's body temperature by doing some gentle jogging that becomes a little more intense as it goes on. As a team, go through some loosening exercises and ensure that everyone gets involved. This does not mean just going through the exercises, but also allowing as many players as possible to organise one aspect of the routine under the overall control of the captain or coach. Even the most junior member can then be aware of his role and of the contribution he can make to the team—even before play has started.

Once loose, do some fielding practice. Not only does this add more intensity to the preparation, but it also is more cricket orientated than stretching. Fielding practice can also be of value in this vital area of the game. A player might not suddenly improve as a fielder, but he can get used to the particular conditions at the ground on the day and hopefully will be better able to reach his individual level of ability for that match.

Next, go through specialist preparation. Depending on the facilities available, this might involve batsmen having a session in the nets, bowlers doing the same thing and the wicket-keeper going through his practice routine. Net surfaces of dubious quality are of no benefit to anyone; in such circumstances, batsmen will be better served by taking some throw-downs on any decent surface, while bowlers hone their actions on the outfield, providing there are reliable footholds. Batsmen must be properly attuned to face the first ball, while bowlers must be at peak levels from the outset. If a bowler takes three overs to reach optimal performance, the game can be won or, more often, lost.

It is not enough simply to be ready for the first ball of the match. A player must be prepared for the first ball of any session and stay ready for action throughout that session. It is not easy for a batsman to sit in the pavilion for hours, ready to go in at any moment. A good routine is to relax until you are the next but one to go in. So, number six in the order puts his pads on when the second wicket falls. At the fall of the third wicket, he gets completely ready, deciding whether to wear a sweater, cap, helmet or whatever. From then on, he concentrates solely on his task.

Similarly, a bowler should not get cold and detached in the field when he is not actually bowling. As a waiting bowler, watch individual batsmen to get an idea of how you might get them out if you were bowling to them. Go through some gentle loosening exercises in the field at appropriate moments to prevent stiffening up. It is also important to take in fluids at every opportunity. Dehydration is a major factor in falling performance as fatigue sets in. A suitable intake of energy drinks or even plain water keeps tiredness at bay and maintains concentration levels.

Just as there was a group warm-up at the start of the match, so there should be a team cool-down at the end. After taking account of the level of fatigue, go through some fairly gentle routines that allow the build-up of acids in the body to dissipate and ensure that you will not be stiff a day or two later when you might be required to do the same thing again.

EQUIPMENT

Cricket requires a fair amount of equipment. If you have any doubts about that, just look at the number of equipment manufacturers and suppliers specialising in the game. Of all the equipment used, the bat is undoubtedly the star of the show. More time and money goes into the choice of a bat than any other piece of equipment. How much of that decision-making process is informed? Among the reasons for not choosing a particular bat are these:

- The colours of the manufacturer's logo match the colours on the club sweater.
- The national cricket hero of the moment uses exactly the same bat.
- The bat is a bit big at the moment, but there's room to grow into it.
- It is the cheapest, or most expensive, bat in the shop.

Let's deal with those points in order. Colours have nothing to do with the quality of the bat.

The bat made for an international player will not be the same as one you might buy off the shelf, and there is no guarantee that the bat wielded by a top player was even made by the firm whose logos appear all over it. You cannot play properly if the bat you are using is too big or too heavy. Finally, the price tag does not necessarily indicate quality in either direction.

Instead of falling into these traps, go for a bat that is the right size and, more importantly, the right weight. If you can play imaginary strokes with just your top hand holding the bat, it is probably about right. The bat should pick up well. It should not feel heavy; rather, it almost flies up when you lift it back. A straight grain down the blade is usually a good sign. In general, a narrow grain is considered to be of higher quality than a wide one. Only then does price come into your decision, and only you know what you can afford.

Good footwear is vital for all cricketers, but it is especially important for fast bowlers. Their boots must grip well and support the feet, which are exposed to great strains and pressures. Fast bowlers' boots generally will be sturdier than those worn by batsmen, but it is important that all boots fit well, are comfortable and offer some protection against the ball to prevent injury.

In a hard-ball game, protective equipment is essential. Pads should be substantial enough to afford protection but also allow easy movement so that you can run. Using thigh pads for each leg, arm guards and chest protectors is a matter of individual preference. A box, or protective cup, should not be considered an optional extra. Gloves should not be too bulky but need to protect all parts of your hands and fingers. For youngsters, a helmet is obligatory, but adult batsmen have a choice. More players at all levels are wearing helmets at all times.

Fielders who stand close to the batsman at short leg or silly point may choose to wear helmets, light pads under their trousers and a box. Even wicket-keepers sometimes wear helmets when they are standing up to the wicket, and they all wear pads and a box, along with their gloves. In general, wicket-keeping pads are lighter and shorter than those worn by batsmen because they should not be used often to stop the ball. A wicket-keeper's gloves, however, are the tools of his trade. They are as important to him as a bat is to a batsman, and a top wicket-keeper will have his gloves made to measure with any special features that he requires. If you purchase wicket-keeping gloves in the mass market, make sure they fit as well as possible and offer proper protection along with the inners. Wicket-keeping gloves must be worked in and made flexible before being used in a match.

When you take account of the basic clothing of socks, trousers, shirt, perhaps a long-sleeved and a sleeveless sweater, a tracksuit for warm-up and training wear, and then you add in playing equipment, it is no wonder that specialist cricket bags come equipped with wheels today. Otherwise, a player might strain something carrying his bag between the car park and the pavilion.

One additional item of equipment is the ball. Usually, the home side provides the ball, but not always. A full-size cricket ball weighs 5.5 ounces (0.2 kg); youngsters, whose fingers cannot grip such an object, use a smaller, 4.75-ounce (0.1 kg) ball. Traditionally, the colour for a cricket ball is red, dating back to the days when shepherds used red wax from a ram's raddle to bind the wool together into a ball. Currently, white balls are used in most limited-overs cricket matches when coloured clothing is worn. The white balls are meant to be easier to see, but they soon become dirty. Experiments have taken place using orange, yellow and even pink balls to test their visibility.

RESONURCES

International Cricket Council:
www.icc-cricket.com

Cricket Australia:
www.cricket.com.au

Bangladesh Cricket Board:
www.tigercricket.com

England and Wales Cricket Board:
www.ecb.co.uk

Board of Control for Cricket in India:
bcci.cricket.deepthi.com

New Zealand Cricket:
www.nzcricket.org.nz

Pakistan Cricket Board:
www.pcboard.com.pk

United Cricket Board of South Africa:
www.cricket.co.za

Sri Lanka Cricket:
www.srilankacricket.lk

West Indies Cricket Board:
www.windiescricket.com

Zimbabwe Cricket:
www.zimcricket.org

Basic Bowling

Most cricket coaching books start with batting, because that is the glamorous aspect of the game. Yet at the start of a match, when the umpire calls, 'Play', the bowler is the one who gets proceedings under way by delivering the first ball. Until he does so, the game does not begin. Therefore, bowling is the logical first step on your path to cricket success. Just as the bowler begins the game, *Cricket: Steps to Success* begins by examining the bowler's craft from the outset. Everything else follows from that point.

By reading about the history of the game, you will appreciate that bowling, like cricket itself, has developed over the years. The art of propelling a cricket ball towards a set of stumps 22 yards (20.1 m) away has become a highly co-ordinated athletic pursuit. Whether a fast bowler gallops up to the wicket or a spinner takes just a few paces at a gentle trot, the principles are the same: The bowler wants an action that will give him consistency and, at the same time, prevent injury. Guidelines for avoiding injury are discussed later in this chapter and in The Sport of Cricket. Consistency can be achieved only if the action is simple. If it is, the action can be repeated, and that repetition can produce

the consistency that allows the bowler to exert control over the batsman.

Consistency should not be confused with predictability. It might be argued that if the bowler does not know where the ball is going, what chance does the batsman have? Although that is true, it is possible to make the batsman's life difficult without trying to surprise him with a straight one. Bowlers should strive to control the ball and use the skills associated with their bowling style to confuse the batsman. These skills include pace, swing and seam movement for quicker bowlers, with turn and flight the main weapons in the armoury of the spinners. The two main groups of bowlers, fast bowlers and spinners, are considered in detail in steps 2 and 3.

Whatever the style, the principles of bowling remain the same. Bowling is not necessarily a natural movement. If you listened to biomechanists talking about co-ordinated muscle movements, you will soon come to the conclusion that muscle co-ordination is impossible to achieve. Similarly, if you listened to someone going through the mechanics of breathing and tried to follow the instructions, you would probably asphyxiate! It is important to encourage those with natural ability to progress by polishing their actions until they reach the required level of consistency; it is equally important to help those who are starting from scratch to learn how to bowl. However good you might be already, it is not a bad thing to revisit the basics occasionally to ensure that you have not allowed bad habits to detract from the efficiency of your actions.

DELIVERY

Delivering the ball requires a variety of physical movements, some of which could leave the bowler vulnerable to injury if he is not carefully monitored. For example, safe actions are those that will not increase the risk of injury in what is an explosive physical movement in the case of a fast bowler. The main areas of concern are the lower back, knees and ankles. Some injuries are inevitable, but you can ensure that the risk is kept to a minimum by using the right equipment, warming up thoroughly and ensuring that the action does not put excessive strain on any part of your anatomy. For years, many fast bowlers reached a certain stage of their professional careers when they suffered stress fractures of the lower back. Some recovered with the help of expert medical treatment, but others were forced to leave the game.

To counter the problem, authorities introduced fast bowling directives that were designed to prevent youngsters from being overbowled at a time when their skeletal structure was still maturing. Of course, if young bowlers develop good actions from the outset, such protection should not be necessary. At one time, all bowlers were taught to be side-on when they delivered the ball (figure 1.1a). Then it became acceptable to be chest-on (figure 1.1b). It was said that these were the only two ways of bowling without causing undue stress to the back. Later it was admitted that there was a third acceptable way: 45 degrees (figure 1.1c). In this case, the bowler is neither side-on nor chest-on, but somewhere in between. All this misses the point: Problems occur when the feet, hips and shoulders are not in the same plane. It is safe to be side-on, chest-on or at any of the 88 degrees in between, providing the feet, hips and shoulders are aligned properly. If all three parts of the anatomy conform to the same plane, the bowling action should be safe.

Figure 1.1   **Fast Delivery Styles**

SIDE-ON

1. Back foot parallel to bowling crease
2. Hips and shoulders at right angles to bowling crease
3. Front shoulder and hip pointed at batsman
4. Head poised to lead down the pitch

a

CHEST-ON

1. Feet, hips and shoulders in same plane

b

(continued)

Figure 1.1 *(continued)*

45 DEGREES

1. Feet, hips and shoulders in same plane

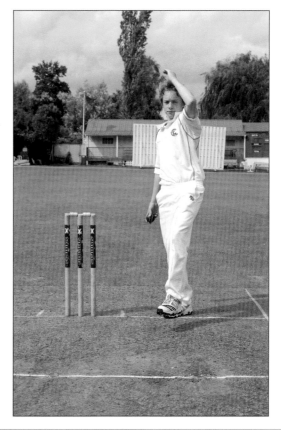

c

Although individual approaches differ, this step concentrates on what has always been considered to be the classical, side-on action. This is not an attempt to produce clones, all bowling in exactly the same manner; rather, it stresses the importance of using a simple action that can be repeated ball after ball, over after over, in order to attain the desired consistency.

Whether you are an experienced bowler starting out on a new season or a new bowler just starting out, certain basics should be followed to ensure that your action is in good order and that you begin with good habits.

To deliver with a side-on action, stand sideways to the target (figure 1.2a), which could be either a mark on a wall or a partner. If you are a right-arm bowler, your left shoulder should point directly at the target with the right shoulder pointing away from it. Bring the hand with the ball in it up under your chin, and then lift your front arm so that it is pointing straight up, with particular emphasis on the section between the shoulder and the elbow. Without lowering this arm, look behind it by arching your back before lifting your front leg, so that you are showing the sole of your foot to the batsman while keeping your back foot parallel to the bowling crease (figure 1.2b).

Figure 1.2   **Stationary Side-On Delivery**

INITIAL STANCE

1. Sideways to target
2. Left shoulder pointing at target (right-arm bowler)
3. Back foot parallel to bowling crease
4. Hold ball in simple standard grip
5. Bring ball under chin
6. Lift front arm
7. Look at batsman from behind front arm

a

FRONT LEG LIFTED

1. Lift front leg
2. Show sole of foot to batsman
3. Keep back foot parallel to bowling crease

b

(continued)

Figure 1.2 *(continued)*

FRONT ARM CHOP

1. Front arm chops down
2. Front arm figuratively splits target in two

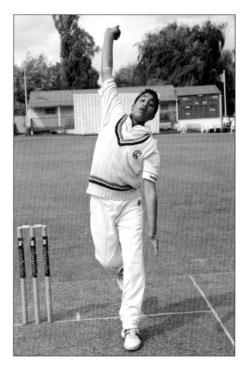

c

ARM PULLS THROUGH

1. Front arm pulls down and through close to body and front leg
2. Bowling arm comes over as high as possible
3. Ball is released to target

d

FOLLOW-THROUGH

1. Bowler's momentum takes him down pitch towards batsman
2. Bowler runs towards off side to prevent damaging pitch

e

From this side-on position, you are ready to bowl. To do so, your front arm effectively chops down as if giving a karate chop to the target, splitting it in two (figure 1.2c). It then travels down past your front leg and is pulled through to finish high behind your head (figure 1.2d). At the same time, your bowling arm follows an identical path, going from under your chin down to the side of your body and then sweeping over as high as possible. Your back leg powers through to become the leading leg, propelling your head towards the target (figure 1.2e).

This might appear as a disjointed set of movements, but even from a standing start, these movements form the basis of sound action. Be careful not to let the heaviest part of your body—your head—fall away to the off side. If you do, your leg will flail out in an attempt to maintain balance instead of adding impetus to the action. In the process, your bowling arm has swept over 12 o'clock high to release the ball at the top of your action, ensuring that you extract any possible bounce from the pitch and, at the same time, helping you bowl straight.

If your head falls away in the action, your brain tries to make an adjustment. It knows the target, the wicket, has not moved, so if your head is moving towards the off side, the target is now to the right. Compensation often results in the ball being fired down the leg side. However, if everything moves in a straight line towards the target, it is likely you will bowl straight. When you are really proficient, you will be able to nominate which stump you are going to hit merely by getting everything moving towards that stump.

Be aware of different parts of your body at particular stages of your action. It is a good idea to warm up before a match by standing at the crease and going through your action a few times without releasing the ball, merely to ensure that your action is working as it should. It sometimes helps to close your eyes while doing this so that you can concentrate on what various parts of your body are doing without being distracted by the scenery. Then, go through the same routine off half a dozen paces before going off your full run and releasing the ball as if for real.

If you are in the process of modifying your action, you will put too much pressure on yourself if you try to make adjustments in a competitive situation. It is best not to make changes in a match. If you usually have the upper hand on a certain batsman in the nets, you will not want to lose that superiority while working on your action, which is a work in progress. To improve, you will probably have to go backwards before going forwards. If you are a fast bowler, don't be discouraged if you lose pace while opening up the opportunity to be even quicker in the future.

To counter these problems, it's a good idea to put a mark on the back of the net at approximately the height above the pitch that the ball would be some 15 yards (13.7 m) along its trajectory. Make the mark big enough to hit with regularity, and then put the stumps from which you deliver the ball 15 yards from the back of the net. In this way, you will not appear to lose any pace while you are making changes to your action—in fact, you will appear to be bowling quicker than ever—and there will be no batsman to take advantage of any waywardness that might be evident before the remodelling of your action is complete.

Make improvements in your own time. Once you are comfortable, gradually move back towards the full 22 yards (20.1 m). At the same time, adjust the mark at the back of the net until, from 22 yards away, you are aiming at a target on the length you are trying to hit. Start with a large target that you can hit easily; gradually decrease the size until it tests you but is not so small as to be demoralising. After you have mastered that target, you can think about bowling at a batsman again and taking your modified action into a match situation.

Misstep
The ball repeatedly goes down the off side.

Correction
Make sure you are set up correctly and your alignment is towards the target rather than too far to the off side. Both these faults can be countered to help you bowl straight and direct balls at the wicket.

Misstep
The ball repeatedly goes down the leg side.

Correction
Keep your head up and moving towards the target during the delivery, rather than falling away.

RUN-UP

You might have been surprised that we dealt with the delivery before the run-up, but if you are prepared to attend to the detail described in the previous section, the honing of the delivery actually takes place before you start to run up to the crease. Why do you need to run in to bowl anyway, especially if you are a spinner?

The answer to that question is that if you are a spinner, you do not really need a run-up. In fact, possibly the greatest spinner in cricket history, Australian leg-break bowler Shane Warne, walked just a couple of paces before jumping into his delivery stride. The key word is jump. If you want to get into the side-on position, you

need to get airborne to change from running or walking straight to the wicket in order to turn your body through 90 degrees.

The other reason for a run-up is to add momentum to your action, especially if you are a quicker bowler. There is a danger that you may run in too quickly, striving for that desirable extra pace. However, no proven formula says that the quicker you approach the wicket, the faster the ball is bowled. In fact, if you are belting into the delivery stride, there is every chance that you will be off balance, will not get the full benefit of the action and will actually lose pace and control. That is why bowlers such as Warne take such a measured approach to the stumps: there is no danger they would not be in total control of their action.

Research conducted at the New Zealand High Performance Centre at Lincoln University, just outside Christchurch, when the Australian players were on tour there found that the speed of Warne's arm in the delivery was in fact quicker than that of his pace-bowling colleague, Glenn McGrath. The difference was that Warne put all his energy into spinning the ball, while McGrath converted his energy into sending the ball down quickly. He would not have been able to do so if he had not been as balanced as Warne, despite running in quicker.

If you have confidence in your action, you will want full benefit from its mechanics and will not want to rush through it too quickly. When you run up to the wicket (figure 1.3*a*), jump high enough to get side-on, ready to deliver (figure 1.3*b* and *c*). As you land on your back foot, bring your bowling hand and the ball up to your chin and point your front arm upwards (figure 1.3*d*). Look behind that front arm and raise your front foot. Does this position sound familiar? It should, because this is exactly how a good action from a standing position was described earlier. That is why it is important even for experienced bowlers to run through the basics every now and then to check that their action is in good order.

Figure 1.3   Run-Up

RUN-UP

1. Start slowly with short strides
2. Lean forward and gather pace with balanced strides
3. Reach top pace as you reach delivery stride

a

(continued)

Figure 1.3   *(continued)*

JUMP

1. Jump into delivery stride

b

TURN

1. Turn 90 degrees in midair
2. Land in the coiled position

c

LAND

1. Land on your back foot
2. Bring front arm upwards
3. Point front arm upwards

d

How far should a bowler run? Although this is personal preference, some basic guidelines are worth considering when you are trying to achieve the right run-up, one that gives you the rhythm to bowl as effectively as possible. Spinners require shorter approaches than pace bowlers, but if a spinner wants to run 5, 7, even 10 paces in order to achieve the rhythm that allows him to arrive at the crease in a balanced position, so be it.

Quicker bowlers may run as a minimum the same distance as a spinner's maximum. If your delivery is built around a strong action with use of your wrist to generate pace, why tire yourself by running 30 yards (27.4 m) when a dozen paces are adequate? On the other hand, if you have the type of action that requires momentum through the crease, it can be more exhausting trying to bowl off 15 paces than off 25. It is pointless to run farther than required, but do not be cajoled into shortening your run below what you are comfortable with.

The important thing is to gather momentum gradually as you approach the wicket. You probably will start with a couple of walking paces before breaking into a trot and gathering pace until just before the delivery stride. Do not try to increase pace through the delivery stride or you will lose your balance. Bear another point in mind: you might come in at a slight angle, but once you are within 4 or 5 yards (3.7 or 4.6 m) of the wicket, you should be running straight towards the target, the stumps that are 22 yards (20.1 m) away. Any deviation means that your run is wasted, and you are building momentum in the wrong direction. Remember that your head is the vital part of your body, and the longer you can keep it going towards the target, the less likely you are to stray from your direction and bowl a bad line.

In the classical side-on delivery, the ball is delivered from close to the stumps. What if you find that such an action does not come naturally, and your feet, hips and shoulders are in one of the other 89-degree planes mentioned at the start of the step? You perhaps can afford to run in a little straighter and not jump as high because you do not need to get side-on. You can run straight through and put all your momentum into the delivery. However, the basic principle remains the same. From your approach to the wicket until natural momentum takes you away to the off side of the pitch before you risk the umpire's wrath by running onto the danger area, make sure your head is going towards the target.

If you manage that, your line should be good enough to eliminate wides. However, you should also do everything you can to avoid overstepping and bowling a no-ball. Both wides and no-balls are known as extras because both add a run to the total without the batsman having to do anything to earn it. A ball is deemed to be a wide when the bowler delivers too far away from the batsman to allow him to reach it with his bat. A no ball occurs when the bowler fails to have at least some part of his front foot behind the popping crease. In these cases, a run is added to the total, and the batsman has a free hit. Because you know that the batsman can only be run-out off a no-ball, why strive for that last fraction of an inch that will make no perceptible difference to the pace of the ball? Sacrifice the final inch or so to make sure you have part of your front foot behind the popping crease. You have yards behind the line in which to land your foot, while a fraction of an inch over it results in a no ball.

Plenty of first-class bowlers have been plagued with no-ball problems, and it seems ridiculous that they did not sort it out early in their careers, or at least have a coach sort it out for them. The process is simple. Start on the popping crease and run backwards away from the pitch. Remember which foot you lead off with and run until you feel comfortable that you have reached optimum speed and are ready to bowl. Go through your action and note where your front foot lands or get a colleague to mark it for you. Pace out from that point to the crease, remember the number of paces and with which foot you led off, add a few inches for safety—and you have your run.

It is important not to look down as you approach the stumps—look at the target. You get some weird replies when you ask a bowler where he looks as he delivers the ball, if he is aware of where he is looking at all. A darts player tends to look at the treble twenty if that is where he is aiming on the board. Why should a bowler be different? The only difference is that the man throwing the darts is not bouncing his arrows before they hit the board. A bowler can concentrate either on where he is pitching the ball or on the target itself, if he is confident that his length will be right, but he must focus on what he is concentrating on, rather than just looking in its general direction. It is good to have a mark somewhere along the run so that you know, as soon as you hit it with a particular foot, that you will be right from there on in. You can concentrate on your action rather than worry about where your feet are going to land.

Misstep

The length of the delivery is not as you would want.

Correction

This usually occurs because you are looking at the wrong spot when delivering. If you are bowling too short, look farther up towards the wicket; if too full, bring your focus back to a point on the pitch nearer you than the batsman.

Concentration is vital for a bowler, but you must focus that concentration only on what you can control. It is no good being distracted by peripheral thoughts. You might have just had a row with a friend, but you cannot resolve it as you run up to bowl. Put it out of your mind. Similarly, you cannot control whether the batsman is right- or left-handed; you might not enjoy bowling to a left-hander, but there is nothing you can do about it. Put it out of your mind. You cannot control the direction of the wind, the slope of the ground, the little niggle in your right knee, whether the captain will give you an extra slip or even the feel of the ball in your hand. Put everything that you cannot control outside your sphere of concentration. You can control the type of delivery you are going to bowl, how you are going to bowl it, where you are going to aim it and where you are going to pitch it. Those are the things on which to concentrate.

This requires intense concentration, and you cannot be expected to maintain it at that level throughout the day or even through a session. Bowl the ball, see where it has gone, make a mental note of what adjustment you need to make to ensure the next one is right and then relax as you walk back to your mark. When you get there, use some sort of trigger mechanism to switch your concentration back on, such as taking a deep breath or taking the grip on the ball, and then start again.

Remember the old adage about not being able to get the last ball back. It is no good getting upset with yourself if the last ball was not what you intended. Make the adjustment and get the next one right. Do not get upset with the batsman if he has played and missed. To do so only shows him that he got to you. Do not get upset with the umpire if he turns down an appeal that is blatantly out, for you hope to have other appeals upheld.

When you are having a bad day, have confidence in yourself to pull it round. You might have 0 for 45 off 12 overs, but a couple of maidens will show that you are not bowling too badly. Then an overconfident batsman goes for a big shot and gets out and, in the next over, the new man in the middle falls across his stumps and is given out leg before wicket (LBW). Another is bowled, and suddenly 3 for 52 off 16 overs looks rather good. The fact is that if you generally take a wicket every 7 overs, and you go 21 overs without taking one, you are putting wickets in the bank for future withdrawal. Adopt the attitude that you are owed 3 wickets from the previous barren spell, not that you may never take a wicket again. Have that confidence and you will avoid the fatal error of trying too hard to produce a magic ball every time you run up to the wicket. Have confidence but be realistic at the same time, and the results will follow.

Basic Bowling Drill 1. *Stationary Bowling to a Target*

Mark an area on a wall about 4 feet high and 2 feet (1.2 m high by .6 m) across. From about 15 yards (13.7 m), bowl at the target from a standing position. Bowl six times.

To Increase Difficulty

- Reduce the size of the target until it is 28 inches high and 9 inches across (71.1 cm high and 23 cm across).

To Decrease Difficulty

- Increase the size of the target until you can score 5 points every time.

Success Check

- Stand side-on to the target.
- Raise front arm upwards.

- Look behind front arm.
- Lift front foot towards target.
- Bring front arm down, splitting target.
- Swing bowling arm over by ear.
- Drive back foot through towards target.
- Move head towards target.

Score Your Success

5 or 6 balls on target = 5 points

3 or 4 balls on target = 3 points

1 or 2 balls on target = 1 point

Your Score ___

Basic Bowling Drill 2. *Run-Up Bowling to a Target*

Mark an area on a wall about 4 feet high and 2 feet across (1.2 m and .6 m). From about 18 yards (16.5 m), bowl at the target from a full run-up. Bowl six times.

To Increase Difficulty

- Reduce the size of the target until it is 28 inches high and 9 inches (71.1 cm and 23 cm) across.
- Increase the length of delivery to 22 yards (20.1 m).

To Decrease Difficulty

- Increase the size of the target until you can score 5 points every time.
- Move closer to the target before delivering the ball.

Success Check

- Establish the length of your run.
- Have a good rhythm, gradually gathering pace as you near the wicket.
- Jump into the delivery position.
- Bowl the ball and follow through towards the target.

Score Your Success

5 or 6 balls on target = 5 points

3 or 4 balls on target = 3 points

1 or 2 balls on target = 1 point

Your Score ___

Basic Bowling Drill 3. *Technique Check*

Mark out your run. Without the ball, run in and execute your bowling motion while someone watches you. Have your observer use the success checks to evaluate your technique. Bowl six times.

Success Check

- Establish the length of your run.
- Develop good rhythm, gradually gathering pace as you near the wicket.

- Jump into the delivery position.
- Bowl the ball and follow through towards the target.

Score Your Success

Bowl 6 balls with sound technique = 5 points

Bowl 4 or 5 balls with sound technique = 3 points

Your Score ___

SUCCESS SUMMARY OF BASIC BOWLING

Remember that the key to successful bowling is a good action; a smooth, rhythmical approach to the wicket; and a jump into the action itself. Make sure you keep your shoulders and hips in the same plane, use your non-bowling arm as a direction finder and follow right through with your head always going towards the target. You want a simple action that can be repeated because this will give you consistency. Concentrate and do not let your attention wander. And want to bowl. You cannot take wickets unless you are bowling.

Before moving on to step 2, Fast Bowling, or step 3, Spin Bowling, evaluate how you did on the basic bowling drills in this step. Tally your scores to determine how well you have mastered the skill of basic bowling. If you scored at least 8 points, you are ready to move on. If you did not score at least 8 points, practice the drills again until you raise your scores before moving on.

Basic Bowling Drills

1. Stationary Bowling to a Target	___ out of 5
2. Run-Up Bowling to a Target	___ out of 5
3. Technique Check	___ out of 5
Total	___ *out of 15*

Once you have mastered basic bowling, you will want to specialise in the style of bowling that will suit you best. You might want to be a fast bowler with the associated thrill of seeing the stumps flying. In step 2, Fast Bowling, you will learn what is required to be a quick bowler who demands respect from all batsmen because of the physical threat posed to them. Or you might become a medium-pace bowler who relies on control and movement to take wickets. On the other hand, the prospect of becoming a spin bowler might appeal to you, in which case move on to step 3. There, you will learn all about flight and turn, and you will derive your satisfaction not from brute force but from deception and from testing the batsman's patience.

Whichever style you opt for now, you are not compelled to bowl that way forever. You might try your hand at being a fast bowler, but if you find it is not for you, have a go at spin bowling instead. You might want to move in the opposite direction, so it would be a good idea to go through steps 2 and 3 to discover what suits you best. Both styles require a good basic action, so if you have mastered step 1, you are in a good position to make rapid strides from here.

Fast Bowling

Fast bowlers are the kings of cricket. Batsmen might hog the glamour, and spinners might beguile with their craft, but the genuine quickie rules the roost. A successful off-spinning all-rounder playing for Oxford University once remarked, 'I so wish I was a fast bowler. Nobody would bowl bouncers at me when I was batting and everyone would treat me with respect.' It is easy to sympathise, for with their ability to break wickets and bones, fast bowlers bend the knee to no one in the game, at least when they bowl well. But if they are wayward, a good batsman will simply pick off the bad balls and use the pace to help the ball speed to the boundary.

Because everything in the delivery moves quickly, it is absolutely vital that you get your action right as a fast bowler. If you are slightly out of synchronisation, pace will be lost. If you fail to apply the basics, any faults will be magnified with spectacularly bad results and, quite possibly, injury if the faulty action is allowed to continue. In addition to the possibility of injury to the batsman, caused by the sheer pace of the ball hitting him, there is a serious risk to you, the bowler.

You need to be fit if you are going to deliver the ball at real speed. Bowling places great strains on the body, and the impact pressures are immense. Look at a still photograph of a fast bowler at the moment of delivery, and you will see that he is straining every sinew (figure 2.1). Unless you are physically prepared and properly warmed up, something is going to give, hence the importance of a good action that will not increase the strain on any part of your body.

Figure 2.1　A fast bowler puts a lot of strain on his body.

Despite the effort that goes into bowling quickly, the very best do not betray the strain but seem to glide in to the wicket and deliver the ball with silky smoothness. Their pace does involve effort, but their actions are so fluent and their co-ordination is such that the ball flies out of their hands and gives the batsman just a fraction of a second to respond. That is the thrilling spectacle of a great fast bowler at work. A contest with a top batsman contains all the elements that make cricket such a great game: skill from both batsman and bowler and the

bowler's athleticism and physical power pitted against the courage of the batsman.

As a young, aspiring fast bowler at school, I was playing in a match in front of my history master. Next day in class, he turned to me and said, 'Well, my boy, you look like a fast bowler, and you're probably stupid enough to be one!' That is a common misconception. A fast bowler who does not think about his art is probably not a very good fast bowler. Being successful requires thought about how to fully utilise the great gift of speed, and fast bowling is an art as well as sheer physical effort.

Misstep
You fail to generate pace to reflect the effort being expended.
Correction
Ensure that you are using each element of your action.

The faster you are, the more margin for error you have with regard to line and length because the batsman has less time to take advantage of a poor ball. But only the very fastest bowlers can rely on pace to take wickets. Although it is possible to increase your speed by improving your action and physical condition, a naturally fast bowler has the correct physical makeup at

the outset. The majority of bowlers will fall into the fast-medium category and so require other weapons in their armoury if they are to succeed. Swing, seam, change of pace and variation of length are additional means for taking wickets. If you can master all these skills, you will improve your bowling and your understanding that fast bowling is indeed an art.

SWING

Step 1 considered the classical, side-on action of bowling. This action is perfect for encouraging the ball to out-swing or away-swing, making the ball deviate away from a right-handed batsman (figure 2.2). The bowler starts the ball's journey on a leg-stump line, but then tries to hit middle or off. If the ball swings to find the edge of the bat, it can result in a catch to the wicket-keeper or the slip cordon, the row of slips and gulley. More annoyingly for the bowler, the ball can evade the catchers and fly down to the third-man boundary for four. It is one of the perpetual bugbears for the out-swing bowler.

Being side-on is just one of the prerequisites for bowling the away-swinger, but it does not guarantee success by itself. Some bowlers can bowl this ball while being chest-on. Still, a side-

on action gives you the best chance to make the ball move away from the batsman through the air. Even more important is your wrist position at the moment of release, which results from how you grip the ball.

Place the ball in your fingers—never in the palm of your hand—with the seam upright but turned slightly in the direction you want the ball to swing, in this case towards the slips. Your first two fingers are on either side of the seam, while the bottom of the seam rests on the side of your thumb (figure 2.3). This position is important: If you change your grip and have the seam resting on the flat of your thumb, this will radically alter your wrist position, making it virtually impossible to release the ball in the correct way.

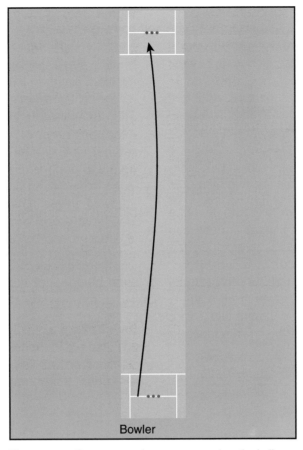

Figure 2.2 On an out-swing, or away-swing, the ball deviates away from a right-handed batsman.

Figure 2.3 **Out-Swing**

GRIP

1. Ball held in fingers, not palm
2. Fingers spaced on either side of seam
3. Seam upright and pointing in direction of intended swing
4. Shiny side of ball is to your right
5. Seam rests on side of thumb
6. Wrist is in position behind ball to help it swing away

19

To help the ball swing, you need to work on it. It is well within the Laws of Cricket to enhance the shine on one side of the ball, providing you use only natural substances, such as the sweat from your face. One reason why a new ball may not swing appreciably is that there has not been time for its two sides to attain differing conditions, one shiny and the other rough. Once it has reached this state, make sure you grip the ball with the shiny side on the outside of the intended curve. As the ball travels down the pitch, the shiny side should be to the right of the seam as you watch it go. To achieve this result, keep the seam upright. If the ball is wobbling, you will not be able to make it swing. The upright seam is a product of your grip.

If you can get a red and white half ball, bowl with it in order to experiment with your grip until you are confident that you can always deliver the ball with the seam upright. Pay attention to how you hold the ball before each delivery. If you don't, the eighth ball you bowl might be perfect, but you might not know what you did to make it so.

It would be easy to become very technical about why a cricket ball swings, but all you need to know is what makes it most likely to swing. Still, humid atmospheric conditions usually help, but because you have no control over the weather, that should not be a focus of your concentration. You can control the angle of the seam, which acts as a sort of rudder as the ball goes through the air. That is a simplification of the aerodynamics involved, as is the statement that the shiny side goes through the air more quickly than the rough side, and so the ball swings away from the shiny side.

These are things that make swing more likely to occur, but they will not be evident unless your action and delivery are right. When you are side-on and using the correct grip, your bowling arm will sweep across your body with your wrist in the right position to encourage the ball to swing. Imagine that you are doing all you can to maintain contact between the ball and your fingers for as long as possible, right down to the last millisecond. Doing so will cause the ball to rotate backwards as it leaves your fingers, and this will enhance the chance of swing. That is all we can aspire to: creating the optimum environment for the ball to behave in the intended manner through the air.

The ball must be pitched up to allow it to swing. If you bang it in halfway down the pitch, there will not be enough time for it to deviate through the air. Bowl it full enough to allow it to swing. Draw the batsman into a drive. The ball will move away at the last minute to find the edge of his bat before flying as a catch to the slip. A late swing to the ball is important, for it is much easier for the batsman if the ball swings from the moment it leaves your hand. An injection of pace, if at all possible, will help the swing of the ball to occur later.

Misstep
You fail to achieve the required accuracy.

Correction
Review your action. You might be striving to bowl too quickly or too slowly, and you might not be allowing your action to go through at a natural pace.

Clever bowlers will adjust the amount of swing so that every ball is not the same. They will also change their pace and the position from which they deliver the ball on the crease, from close to the stumps to near the return crease. Sometimes they will vary the delivery itself: instead of trying to swing the ball away, they will bowl a cutter. Because of the wrist position and the grip, away-swing bowlers find it easier to bowl the off-cutter. (Figure 2.4 shows the grip for the off-cutter.) To do so, impart a downward movement to the shiny side of the ball as you release it by dragging your fingers down that side. This puts a spin on the ball, which will not swing but should go straight until it hits the pitch, at which point it cuts back into the batsman.

Figure 2.4   Grip for off-cutter.

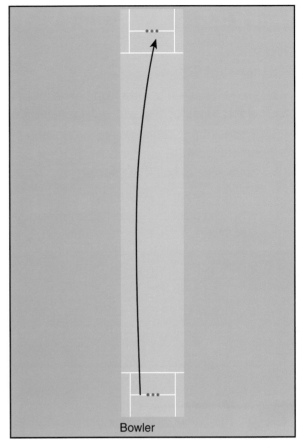

Figure 2.5   On an in-swing fast delivery, the ball deviates towards the right-handed batsman, moving from left to right.

Many of the principles that apply to out-swing also apply to in-swing. As its name suggests, an in-swinger deviates the ball in towards the body of the right-handed batsman, moving from left to right as viewed by the bowler (figure 2.5). In this instance, you do not need to get side-on as you deliver. A slightly open-chested action can help, with your bowling arm not sweeping across your body but perhaps even finishing inside your front leg rather than past the outside.

Your grip on the ball and your wrist position are all-important. The seam should still be up-right, but now it points to the leg side because this is the direction in which you want the ball to swing, from off-stump towards the line of the leg stump. Because you want the ball to swing towards the batsman's body, the shiny side should be to the left of the seam. Just as they are for an away-swing bowl, your fingers should be comfortably spaced on top of and on either side of the seam; at the bottom, the seam should rest on the flat of your thumb (figure 2.6). If you take a ball and change the seam from resting on the side to resting on the flat of your thumb, you will see how the shape of your wrist changes. For the in-swinger, having the ball resting on the flat of your thumb sets the wrist to stay behind the ball and helps it move towards the way you want it to swing.

Figure 2.6   In-Swing

GRIP

1. Ball held in fingers, not palm
2. Fingers spaced to either side of seam but closer together than with out-swinger grip
3. Seam is upright and points in direction of intended swing
4. Shiny side of ball is to your left
5. Seam rests on flat of thumb
6. Wrist is in position behind ball to encourage it to swing in

Misstep

The ball is not swinging or hitting the seam on the pitch.

Correction

Check your grip to ensure that the seam is in the correct position.

Just as the away-swing bowler has a variation in the off-cutter, so the in-swing bowler's grip makes it easier to bowl a leg cutter. (Figure 2.7 shows the grip for the leg cutter.) To do so, drag your fingers down the shiny side of the ball, this time to the left of the seam. This puts a rotation on the ball so that when it pitches, it should dart away from the batsman.

Figure 2.7   Grip for leg cutter.

SEAM

There is a tendency to refer to all pace bowlers as seamers, but there is a distinct difference between those who simply bowl quickly, swing bowlers and seam bowlers. Seamers are those who attempt to confuse batsmen by making the ball pitch on the seam and then move. If the ball moves away from the right-handed batter, there is every chance it will take the outside edge and be caught by the slips or wicket-keeper. If the ball goes the other way, it can go between the bat and the pad to bowl the batsman or hit him on the pad to win an LBW decision.

The big question is, which way will it move? Even the best practitioners of this art don't know which way it will go. Some claim they do, but it is a question of trying to pitch the ball on the seam. If the ball happens to land on one side of the seam, it will go one way; if the ball lands on the other, it will go in the opposite direction. This is a fine line, and no bowler, however good, can be accurate enough to determine which edge of the seam will hit the ground first.

As a bowler, all you can do is ensure that the seam goes through the air in an upright position, and then let the ball and the pitch do the rest. Hold the ball with the seam between your first two fingers at an angle that propels it through the air in an upright position (figure 2.8). The height of your arm in the delivery will affect the ball's movement, so it requires plenty of practice to find the optimum angle to guarantee the ball pitches the way you want. The higher your bowling arm in the delivery, the greater consistency you are likely to experience, and the higher the bounce you will get. Bounce and movement off the seam are more effective than movement on its own.

Figure 2.8 Hold the ball with the seam between first two fingers to propel the ball through the air in an upright position.

Misstep
You fail to get sufficient bounce.

Correction
Stand tall in the delivery and bowl the ball into the pitch rather than just skidding it through.

Just as swing bowlers require favourable conditions to have the best chance of success, so do seamers. The best condition is a pitch that allows the seam to bite and then offers some bounce. A typical English green pitch is ideal, which is why seamers have been so successful in England.

YORKERS, BOUNCERS AND OTHER TRICKS

Fast bowlers do not rely solely on pace and movement either through the air or off the pitch to get their wickets. They have other ways of deceiving batsman, which is why the fast bowler's art is just as practised as that of a spinner. In addition to using the cutters mentioned earlier, a fast bowler has several other ways to unsettle batsmen and take wickets.

The yorker is a delivery that is pitched right up to the batsman and lands at his feet. When this happens, there is every possibility the batsman will play over the top of it. The delivery might initially appear as a half volley or full toss, just ripe for driving; in reality, an attempted drive is likely to find the bat passing over the ball. Because the ball does not bounce, it gets to the batsman sooner than he thinks it will. Since the ball is in its trajectory through the air longer than the standard pitch, it has more chance to swing. The fast, swinging yorker is one of the most difficult balls to counter: The batsman often jabs down on it at the last minute if he makes contact at all.

Because there is such a fine margin of error, practice this delivery in the nets before attempting it in the middle. If the pitch is too full, it is indeed a full toss. If the pitch is a fraction short of yorker length, it becomes a half volley that deserves to be driven. To achieve the right length, it might help to look a little farther ahead towards the target so that you release the ball at the right time in the action. For instance, if you usually look at the point on the pitch where you want the standard ball to land, try looking at the batsman's feet. If you normally look at the base of the stumps, look at a point halfway up the middle.

A good ploy is to bowl a yorker straight after a bouncer, which tests the batsman's courage as well as his technique. The bouncer is banged into the pitch short of a length, with the idea that the steeper trajectory will get the ball to rise higher than from a normal length. But the ball has to be well directed, for a bouncer that is not close enough to the batsman to cause him concern is a wasted ball. Although most batsmen will happily watch bouncers pass wide of the off-stump or harmlessly down the leg side, a bouncer steepling towards a batsman's head or throat is an entirely different matter. The bouncer must not be too wide, but neither can it be so short that it climbs way over the batsman's head. A bouncer or two that shake up the batsman might get him on his back foot or even force him to back away. If either of these happens, the batsman is vulnerable to the yorker.

It might sound strange, but one of the most potent weapons in the fast bowler's armoury is the slower ball. The batsman will find it difficult to adjust to the odd ball that arrives at a reduced pace, and he might well be through his shot before the ball arrives. Bowl the ball straight to hit the stumps if the batsman misses, or have him LBW. Even if the ball is slightly off line, the batsman might find himself hitting the ball in the air to offer a catch, so the delivery has plenty of potential as a wicket-taker.

Disguise is the key. If the ball is obviously slower, the batsman will have little difficulty adjusting. Your arm should come over at the same speed as usual. Vary your grip to bring the ball out of your hand more slowly. Putting three fingers on the ball instead of two, holding the ball farther into your hand rather than with your fingers or using a spinner's grip to deliver the ball with an off-break action will all produce the desired effect (figure 2.9, *a-c*). Bowling with a leg-break action will have the same effect as well, but that requires a high degree of control and is difficult to conceal—even though spotting it is one thing, and playing it is quite another. Some bowlers have more than one way of bowling a slower ball; that can lure a batsman into trouble if he thinks he can detect the slower ball from the bowler's action, only to discover that there is another variety with which to cope.

These deceptive deliveries distinguish the very good fast bowler from the ordinary one. They require much practise to perfect, but when they have been mastered, the rewards justify the effort that goes into getting them right. Stupid enough to be a fast bowler? I don't think I was ever bright enough.

a   b   c

Figure 2.9   Three ways to pitch a slower ball: *(a)* grip the ball with three fingers instead of two; *(b)* hold the ball farther into the hand; and *(c)* use a spinner's grip to deliver the ball with an off-break action.

Fast Bowling Drill 1.   *Technique Check*

Mark out your run. Without the ball, run in and execute your bowling action while someone watches you. Have your observer use the following success checks to evaluate your technique. Bowl six times.

- Make sure your front foot lands with some part behind the popping crease.
- Follow through, moving off the pitch as you do so.

Success Check

- Hit your mark with the same foot each time.
- Gradually increase momentum as you approach the crease.
- Don't look down once you have hit your mark.
- Go through your bowling action, making sure that your feet, hips and shoulders are in the same plane.

Score Your Success

Bowl 6 balls without a no ball = 5 points

Bowl 5 balls without a no ball = 1 point

Bowl 4 balls or fewer without a no ball = 0 points

Your Score ___

Fast Bowling Drill 2.   *Out-Swing Bowling*

Using a red-and-white-halved ball, bowl out-swingers. Make sure the seam stays upright and that the ball swings in the intended direction. Bowl six times.

To Increase Difficulty

- Put down a target and ensure you hit it as well as make the ball swing away.

To Decrease Difficulty

- Remove the target and just make sure the ball swings away as intended.

Success Check

- Grip the ball correctly, with the seam upright and pointing in the intended direction of the swing.

- Rest the seam on the side of your thumb, with your fingers spread to either side on the top of the seam.
- Get side-on and sweep your bowling arm across your body.

Score Your Success

5 or 6 balls bowled with the seam upright = 5 points

3 or 4 balls bowled with the seam upright = 3 points

1 or 2 balls bowled with the seam upright = 1 point

Your Score ___

Fast Bowling Drill 3.   *In-Swing Bowling*

Using a red-and-white-halved ball, bowl in-swingers. Make sure the seam stays upright and the ball swings in the intended direction. Bowl six times.

To Increase Difficulty

- Put down a target and ensure you hit it as well as make the ball swing in.

To Decrease Difficulty

- Remove the target and just make sure the ball swings in the intended direction.

Success Check

- Grip the ball correctly, with the seam upright and pointing in the intended direction of the swing.

- Rest the seam on the flat of your thumb, with your fingers on either side on the top of the seam.
- Try bowling from more of a front-on action, with your bowling arm coming over in front of your body rather than across it.

Score Your Success

5 or 6 balls bowled with the seam upright = 5 points

3 or 4 balls bowled with the seam upright = 3 points

1 or 2 balls bowled with the seam upright = 1 point

Your Score ___

Fast Bowling Drill 4. *Seam Bowling*

Using a red-and-white-halved ball, bowl deliveries making sure the ball pitches on the seam. Bowl six times.

To Increase Difficulty

- Put down a target and ensure you hit it as well as make the ball deviate off the seam.

To Decrease Difficulty

- Remove the target and just make sure the ball deviates off the seam on the pitch.

Success Check

- Grip the ball correctly: seam upright with your fingers on either side of the seam.

- Make sure you deliver the ball with a high bowling arm in order to extract as much bounce as possible.
- Use your action to get as much height as possible.

Score Your Success

5 or 6 balls bowled so the ball pitches on the seam = 5 points

3 or 4 balls bowled so the ball pitches on the seam = 3 points

1 or 2 balls bowled so the ball pitches on the seam =1 point

Your Score ___

Fast Bowling Drill 5. *Slower Balls*

Bowl slower balls without changing your normal action. Use one of the grip changes explained in the text. Bowl six times.

To Increase Difficulty

- Put down a target and ensure you hit it as well as bowl slower balls.

To Decrease Difficulty

- Remove the target and just make sure the ball is a disguised slower ball.

Success Check

- Grip the ball correctly, either with the ball held in the palm of your hand, with three fingers instead of two on top of the ball or with a spinner's grip.

- Make sure you deliver the ball with a normal action rather than with an obvious variation.

Score Your Success

5 or 6 balls bowled as disguised slower balls = 5 points

3 or 4 balls bowled as disguised slower balls = 3 points

1 or 2 balls bowled as disguised slower balls = 1 point

Your Score ___

Fast Bowling Drill 6. *Yorkers*

Bowl a yorker, landing the ball on the popping crease. Bowl six balls.

To Increase Difficulty

- Try to aim each ball directly at the middle stump rather than at the wicket as a whole.

To Decrease Difficulty

- Bowl the ball to hit one of the three stumps.

Success Check

- Run up to bowl with the idea of bowling a yorker.
- Go through your usual delivery action.

- Try to pitch the ball on the popping crease and straight at the stumps.
- Adjust your point of focus until you can land the ball on the popping crease.

Score Your Success

Bowl 6 balls that land on the popping crease = 5 points

Bowl 4 or 5 balls that land on the popping crease = 3 points

Bowl 1 to 3 balls that land on the popping crease = 1 point

Your Score ____

Fast Bowling Drill 7. *Bouncers*

Bowl a bouncer with the goal of getting the ball to bounce above an imaginary batsman's shoulder. Bowl six balls.

To Increase Difficulty

- Bowl each bouncer so that it goes within an imaginary box a foot (.3 m) to either side and above or below a batsman's head.

To Decrease Difficulty

- Just try to get the ball to bounce and be within reach of a batsman.

Success Check

- Run in with your normal approach.
- Bowl quickly and with a high action.

- Try to pitch the ball halfway down the pitch.
- Follow through so that you get the maximum effect from your action.

Score Your Success

Bowl 6 balls that bounce to shoulder height = 5 points

Bowl 4 or 5 balls that bounce to shoulder height = 3 points

Bowl 1 to 3 balls that bounce to shoulder height = 1 point

Your Score ____

Fast Bowling Drill 8. *Mix It Up*

Bowl six balls to a batsman who plays each ball on merit. Each ball should be a different type of bowling. The first ball should be an in-swinger or out-swinger, depending on your normal style. Bowl the second ball with the seam upright so that it lands on the seam. The third ball should be a cutter, either an off-cutter or a leg cutter, whichever you find easiest to bowl. For the fourth ball, bowl a slower ball, disguising it so the batsman cannot detect it. Bowl a bouncer for the fifth ball, getting it to bounce to shoulder height. Finally, deliver a yorker to the batsman's feet, bowling it straight.

To Increase Difficulty

- Bowl every ball at maximum pace while maintaining accuracy.

To Decrease Difficulty

- Reduce your pace but make sure that the ball behaves as intended.

Success Check

- Run up and bowl without changing your normal action.

- When you bowl the second ball with the seam upright, make sure it lands on the seam.
- Disguise the fourth ball so the batsman cannot detect it.
- Make the fifth ball, the bouncer, bounce to shoulder height.
- Bowl the final ball, the yorker, straight so it lands at the batsman's feet.

Score Your Success

Bowl 6 balls that do what they were meant to do = 5 points

Bowl 4 or 5 balls that do what they were meant to do = 3 points

Bowl 1 to 3 balls that do what they were meant to do = 1 point

Your Score ___

SUCCESS SUMMARY OF FAST BOWLING

Remember that fast bowling takes a lot of physical effort, but it is not just the result of brute force. You need the skills described in this step. Make sure you have a smooth, rhythmical run-up, and that you have a sound action that is not going to cause injury. Use all your height to get bounce and then follow through. Check your grip for the type of delivery you are going to bowl.

Decide which is your stock delivery and bowl that way 17 balls out of 18, but occasionally try a variation, such as a cutter, seamer, slow ball, yorker or bouncer. You can even try to swing it the opposite way from how you normally bowl, but the important thing is to not overdo the variations, or the batsman will not be surprised by them.

Before moving on, evaluate how you did on the fast bowling drills in this step. Tally your scores to determine how well you have mastered the skill of fast bowling. If you scored at least 25 points, you are ready to move on. If you did not score at least 25 points, practice the drills again until you raise your scores before progressing.

Fast Bowling Drills

1. Technique Check   ___ out of 5
2. Out-Swing Bowling   ___ out of 5
3. In-Swing Bowling   ___ out of 5
4. Seam Bowling   ___ out of 5
5. Slower Balls   ___ out of 5
6. Yorkers   ___ out of 5
7. Bouncers   ___ out of 5
8. Mix It Up   ___ out of 5

Total   **___ out of 40**

If you master the art of fast bowling—and it is an art—you will not want to consider spin bowling in step 3. You will be too enthralled by the power at your fingertips. However, if you have found fast bowling is not for you, give step 3 your full attention. You might find that you are a natural spin bowler. Even if you are going to be a fast bowler, it might be a good idea to see what step 3 has to offer. You could find that you are an even better spin bowler than fast bowler. At worst, you will learn a little bit about the art of spin, and that will stand you in good stead as you head for step 4. And everyone has to bat, against the spin bowlers as well as the quicks.

Spin Bowling

Once the opening bowlers have done their stuff, and the third and possibly fourth seamers have had a go, the attack is usually placed in the hands of the spinners. This is not to denigrate their role or to establish some sort of pecking order, but is merely the best way to utilise bowling resources. When the shine has gone from the ball and the pace bowlers have become less effective, the spinners come into their own.

If the pitch is one that encourages spin, the pace bowlers might well have to give way earlier. This strategy can help the spinners in that they benefit from bounce, which can be as potent a weapon as turn. They are more likely to achieve it with a newer, harder ball than with one that has been battered into a soft state. This is where a captain who understands the game is required. Without one, spin bowlers often are employed as a last resort and tossed the ball when all else has failed. Doing so undervalues the spin bowlers and reveals a total lack of appreciation for their potency.

The fast bowler comes thundering up to the wicket and hurls the ball down at great pace; the spin bowler employs more subtle tactics.

There is not the dramatic sight of stumps being knocked out of the ground. Instead of power and pace, there is flight and subtlety. If you are bowled as a batsman, it matters not whether the stumps have gone flying through the air or a single bail has dropped to the ground—you are still out bowled.

Because they employ different, more cerebral methods to defeat the batsmen, spin bowlers often take longer to mature and reach their peak. A fast bowler might get away with youthful exuberance to blast batsmen out, but the spinner cannot rely on physical attributes to take wickets. Instead, he must learn his craft thoroughly and develop enough control to ensure he can outwit and eventually snare a batsman. Different qualities are demanded of the spinner, but that does not mean he should be passive or subservient. It is often said of a spin bowler that he possesses the attitude of a fast bowler: He approaches his job aggressively. If that aggression can be harnessed, a spin bowler can be mightily effective by conserving runs and taking wickets. It is no coincidence that the three leading wicket-takers in the history of Test cricket are all spinners.

OFF-SPIN

Right-arm spinners who turn the ball from off to leg are known as off-spinners. They are also sometimes referred to as finger spinners because they use their fingers to impart the required revolutions on the ball as it leaves the hand. When their action is examined in greater detail, this might be the truth, but it is not the whole truth: It is not only the fingers that contribute to turning the ball. From the feet to the fingers, most of the body is involved.

A spin bowler holds the ball in the first two fingers, which should be spread as far apart as possible, tips gripping the seam and the index finger bent from the first joint (figure 3.1). Contrary to what many people think, the thumb plays no part in the action. It can rest lightly on the ball if absolutely necessary, but it should not be used to try to impart spin. The thumb is inflexible compared with other digits, and so it acts more as a brake than a lever to spin the ball.

You generate spin by straightening that crooked index finger and then flicking both fingers in a clockwise direction as the ball leaves your hand. To achieve maximum rotation, your fingers cannot operate on their own. Turn your whole hand as if it were opening a door. The palm of your hand faces downwards initially, with your fingers on top of the ball; after the release, your hand should face upwards.

It is important that the ball revolves on an axis that will result in it pitching on the seam. If the ball lands on its smooth part, it will not have the same traction as when the rough seam makes contact with the pitch, and so it will not turn as much. The smooth part slides while the seam grips the surface. To ensure that this happens consistently, practice with a red-and-white-halved ball. Adjust your grip so that as the ball travels towards the batsman, you can see only one colour. If the ball is a blur of red and white, it is unlikely to pitch on the seam. If you see just red or white, that means the ball is spinning with the seam upright and at right angles to the line of flight, guaranteeing that the ball pitches on the seam.

How do your feet play a part in this action? The answer is that to be effective, the ball should be bowled from the highest point possible in order to achieve maximum bounce. This cannot be achieved with a long delivery stride because the wider the base, the lower the hand will be at the top of the action. Keep your delivery stride short, with your feet landing as close together as is comfortable, but wide enough apart to ensure balance (figure 3.2, a-d).

Figure 3.1 Grip for an off-spin bowler: ball held in first two fingers, tips gripping seam and index finger bent from first joint.

Figure 3.2   Bowling an Off-Break

GRIP

1. Hold ball between first two fingers
2. Spread first two fingers as wide as comfortable along seam
3. Keep index finger bent, ready to straighten to increase spin
4. Keep thumb away from ball; it plays no part in action
5. Position wrist to the right to add to turn

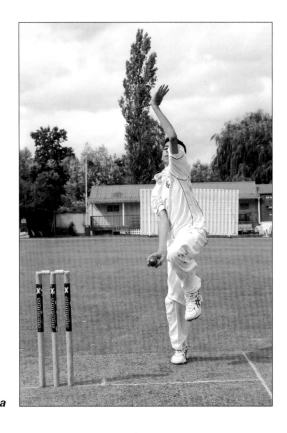

a

DELIVERY

1. Deliver ball from over a short stride
2. Position front foot slightly to the leg side of straight
3. Point toes towards fine leg
4. Hold bowling arm not quite upright
5. Hold head high
6. Deliver ball with momentum towards batsman

b

(continued)

Figure 3.2 *(continued)*

FOLLOW-THROUGH

1. Pivot on front foot
2. Move hips and shoulders in same plane

c

PREPARE TO FIELD

1. Move off pitch quickly after releasing ball
2. After bowling, take position to take advantage of any caught and bowled chance

d

Misstep
You fail to get over the front leg when bowling off-breaks.

Correction
Take a shorter delivery stride.

Once your front foot lands, your whole body should pivot around and over it because that enhances the spinning action of the ball as it leaves the hand. Moving your shoulders and hips add to the sense of your body pivoting around the front foot, achieving more turn without requiring more forced finger action, which could lead to a loss of control. After your back leg has driven through to finish straight down the pitch, your body will have gone through 180 degrees, and the spikes on your front foot should have inscribed a circle in the turf.

Turn and bounce are two of the off-spinner's weapons, but there are others. Off-spinners also use flight. This means that the ball travels in a looping trajectory towards the batsman, rather than inscribing a regular parabola through the air. Flight will be achieved only if you bowl the ball with plenty of revolutions on it and a vigorous action. Then it will travel along a regular path but dip as it reaches the batsman (figure 3.3, *a* and *b*), causing him to misjudge the length. Without that vigorous action, if the ball is given more air or bowled on a higher trajectory, it will merely be a lob without the element of deception.

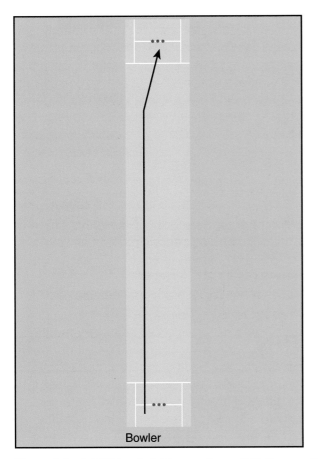

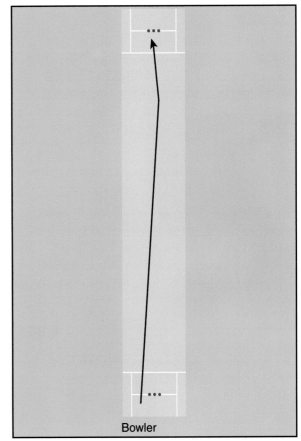

Figure 3.3 *(a)* Off-break right-arm spinner; *(b)* left-arm orthodox.

Misstep
The ball lacks turn when you bowl off-breaks.

Correction
Check your grip and action to see if you are giving yourself the best chance of getting turn.

In addition to spinning or flighting some balls more than others, you can employ another simple variation. Instead of flicking your fingers down the side of the ball as it is released, adjust your grip as if bowling an away-swinger. With no perceivable change of action, the ball will drift away from the batsman through the air rather than spinning back into the batsman off the pitch, often resulting in an outside edge to the wicket-keeper or to the slip.

Like everything else you bowl as an off-spinner, the arm ball or floater needs to be perfected before using it in a match. (Figure 3.4 shows the grip for the floater.) You need to perfect your delivery. Deliberately bowl the delivery to ensure that the ball lands on the smooth part rather than the seam. Release the ball with the seam parallel to the ground rather than at right angles to it. The ball will still spin around the seam and appear to be a standard delivery, but without the same grip on the pitch, it will go straight on.

Figure 3.4 Grip for floater.

Misstep
The batsman spots the arm ball.

Correction
Make sure you bowl the arm ball with the same action as the off-break.

It takes time, practice and patience before you can learn all the off-spinner's tricks and achieve control before you step up with confidence against a batsman in full flow. Sometimes you will be bowling on pitches that assist you, but more often, the surfaces on which you have to operate will be unresponsive. That is when you have to rely on experience and your craft to take wickets.

LEG SPIN

Leg spinners, also known as wrist spinners, turn the ball from leg to off (figure 3.5). The wrist action imparts most of the spin on the ball. If the off-break delivery appears complex, it is nothing compared to the leg-break delivery (figure 3.6, *a-c*). The leg-break delivery takes a longer period to master, but when perfected, it brings with it a high degree of satisfaction. A good leg spinner has the opportunity to make a complete fool of an otherwise competent batsman.

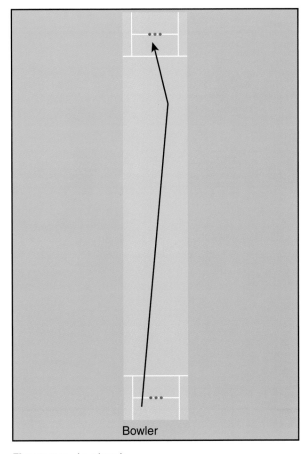

Figure 3.5 Leg break.

Figure 3.6   Bowling a Leg Break

GRIP

1. Use thumb and first two fingers to form a cup for the ball

2. Rest seam along fingertips

3. Keep third finger bent, then straighten it in delivery to impart extra revolutions on ball

4. Cock wrist, ready to flick fingers over top of ball as it is released

a

(continued)

37

Figure 3.6 *(continued)*

DELIVERY

1. Hold bowling arm high
2. Align feet straight down pitch
3. Assume side-on position
4. Deliver ball with high arm

b

FOLLOW-THROUGH

1. Bring bowling arm over quickly
2. Keep head upright and follow ball down pitch until natural momentum takes you away to the off side
3. After delivering the ball, take a position ready for a caught and bowled chance

c

Misstep
The ball lacks turn when you bowl a leg break.

Correction
Check your grip and action to ensure that you are giving yourself the best chance of getting turn.

For the basic leg-spinner's grip, hold the ball in your cupped hand with your thumb and first two fingers extended, and your ring and little finger bent into your palm (figure 3.7). The ball rests with the seam running along the ring finger; this is the finger that straightens as the wrist flicks on release, while the other two fingers snap over the seam. With practice, you'll be able to have the ball come out with the seam at right angles to the line of flight, spinning rapidly so that all purchase can be obtained from the ball pitching on the seam.

Your bowling arm needs to strike through to give enough energy to your wrist as it flicks over the ball. At the end of an over, a leg spinner should be puffing a bit, not because he is unfit but because he has put a great deal of effort into his bowling. The greatest leg spinner of them all, Australia's Shane Warne, certainly put in the effort, yet he would walk just a few paces up to the wicket and then bowl. He made sure that once

he reached the stumps, everything was moving in a straight line towards the target. As a result, he could concentrate on what ball he was going to bowl and put all his effort into that, rather than having to correct any misdirection in his run.

When you put as many revolutions on the ball as Warne, the ball will dip into the batsman as it moves through the air and then will fizz away off the pitch. That is the standard delivery of the leg-break bowler, but top leg-spinners have so many more variations at their disposal. The most common of these is the googly (figure 3.8), a delivery that appears as if it is going to

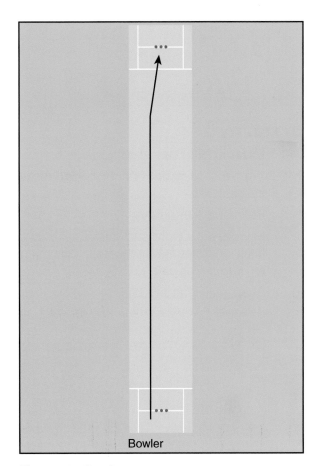

Figure 3.8 Googly.

Figure 3.7 Grip for leg break.

turn as a leg break, from leg to off, but in fact goes the other way (figure 3.9, *a* and *b*). This is achieved by turning your wrist around during delivery so that the back of your bowling hand faces the batsman. The ball comes out over the tips of your fingers, rather than out of your hand as the fingers spin over the top. By turning your wrist so far around, the same movement of the fingers produces turn in the other direction. To ensure that your wrist can get into this position, it sometimes helps to drop your left shoulder a little in delivery. Be careful with this because doing so does make it a little more obvious to the batsman that something different is coming.

Figure 3.9   Googly

GRIP

1. Use thumb and first two fingers to form a cup for the ball
2. Rest seam along fingertips
3. Keep third finger bent, then straighten in delivery to impart extra revolutions on ball
4. Cock wrist, ready to flick fingers over top of ball as it is released

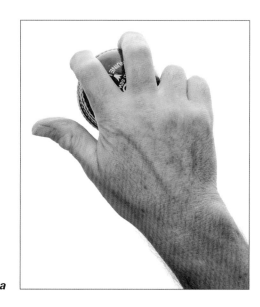

a

DELIVERY

1. Lower left shoulder slightly
2. Turn wrist so back of bowling hand faces batsman
3. Bring arm over quickly
4. Keep head upright and follow ball down pitch until natural momentum takes you away to the off side
5. After delivering the ball, take a position ready for a caught and bowled chance

b

Misstep
You are unable to bowl a googly.

Correction
Try dropping your front shoulder in the delivery stride to get your wrist into the correct position.

Deception is all part of the craft, which is why good leg-spin bowlers might be able to bowl more than one type of googly. There is the googly you use at first, which the batsman learns to recognise, and then there is the one you disguise in a different way. Just as the batsman has learnt to pick whether it is a leg break or googly coming towards him, you slip in the other googly to ensure that confusion reigns in the batsman's mind.

Warne, among others, played on this uncertainty by announcing that he had just developed a new mystery ball. He might have done so, or he might not, but if the batsman was looking for something new, Warne had established doubt and fear in his opponent's mind. Warne was, however, master of all the deceptions going. He bowled the top spinner (figure 3.10 shows the grip for the top spinner), which has the fingers

snapping over the ball as it comes out of the side of the hand and has the spin going straight down the pitch. This delivery is particularly effective in trapping batsmen LBW because it goes straight on rather than turning.

So, too, is the flipper (figure 3.11). This is bowled like a top spinner, but instead of your fingers putting overspin on the ball as it leaves your hand, they flick the other way so they

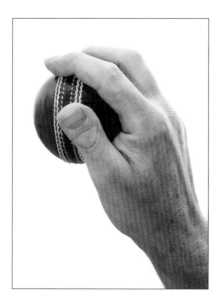

Figure 3.10 Grip for top spinner.

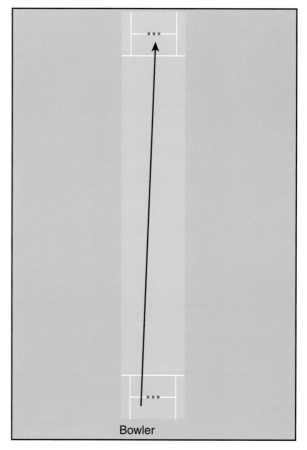
Bowler

Figure 3.11 Flipper.

underspin the ball (figure 3.12). Like the top spinner, this ball goes straight on but has the added benefit of keeping low on pitching. So why bowl the top spinner if the flipper is potentially more difficult for the batter to play?

The answer is that the flipper is also more difficult to bowl. This dilemma sums up leg-spin bowling as a whole. It is an exacting art to master but offers great rewards to those who reach the highest level.

Figure 3.12   Flipper

GRIP

1. Use first two fingers to form a cup for the ball
2. Bend thumb back under seam
3. Bend third finger, then straighten it in delivery to impart extra revolutions on ball
4. Cock wrist, ready for thumb to flick forward under ball as it is released

LEFT-ARM SPIN

Left-arm spinners warrant special mention because of the variation they bring to an attack. Their skills are directly mirrored in the right-arm spin bowler (figure 3.13, *a-c*), but the fact that the same action turns the ball in the opposite direction poses different problems for the batsman. For example, a left-arm finger spinner, bowling with a right-arm bowler's action, will turn the ball from leg to off. It means that he can enjoy all the control associated with being a finger spinner, but he still turn the ball away from the batsman and can exploit all the angles.

A left-arm spinner can attack the batsman by bowling around the wicket or delivering the ball from the left-hand side of the stumps as he looks down the pitch. If the ball is turning, he can pitch it in line with the stumps and straighten it to have the batsman LBW or bowled. If the left-arm spinner pitches it on off-stump or just outside, the batsman has to play it in case it does not turn and carries on to bowl him. However, if it does turn, there is every chance that it will find the edge, resulting in a catch to the slip or wicket-keeper.

If a left-arm spinner wants to keep the batsmen quiet, he can bowl over the wicket and pitch the ball in the footmarks created by a right-arm, over-the-wicket bowler at the other end. With the ball generally pitching outside leg-stump, there is no chance of an LBW; therefore, the batsman should not be bowled. Even so, it lays down the challenge to the batsman to attack the bowling. With uneven bounce and turn out of the rough, this can prove to be dangerous. It comes down to who has the greater patience, batsman or bowler.

Figure 3.13 **Left-Arm Spin**

PREPARATION

1. Grip ball in left hand
2. Raise right arm
3. Lift right foot

a

EXECUTION

1. Right arm chops through
2. Left arm brings ball over
3. Front foot pivots
4. Left leg drives through

b

(continued)

Figure 3.13 *(continued)*

FOLLOW-THROUGH

1. Left arm follows through naturally after release
2. Move off pitch quickly after releasing ball

c

Good left-arm wrist spinners also provide problems for batsmen, in a similar way to their right-arm, leg-spinning colleagues. But just like leg spinners, chinaman (the name given to a left-arm wrist spinner who bowls the standard delivery; see figure 3.14) and googly bowlers have a demanding job gaining enough control and consistency to be really effective. However, the end results make all the hours of practice worthwhile.

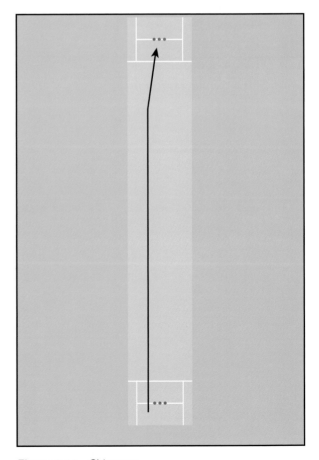

Figure 3.14 Chinaman.

Spin Bowling Drill 1. *Off-Break Bowling*

Using a red-and-white-halved ball, bowl six off-breaks. Make sure you can see only one colour as the ball goes towards the batsman.

To Increase Difficulty

- Place a target progressively further outside off-stump and turn the ball back to hit the stumps.

To Decrease Difficulty

- Place a target close to the stumps so you have to turn the ball only slightly to hit the stumps.

Success Check

- Grip the ball correctly, with your first two fingers spread along the seam.
- Make sure that your thumb does not impede the spin.

- Take a short delivery stride and pivot on your front foot as you bowl.
- Reinforce the spin from your fingers by turning your whole hand as you release the ball.
- At the completion of the action, your body should have turned 180 degrees so what was your bowling shoulder is now pointing at the target.

Score Your Success

5 or 6 balls turn from off to leg = 5 points

3 or 4 balls turn from off to leg = 3 points

1 or 2 balls turn from off to leg = 1 point

Your Score ___

Spin Bowling Drill 2. *Leg-Break Bowling*

Using a red-and-white-halved ball, bowl six leg breaks. Make sure you can see only one colour as the ball goes towards the batsman.

To Increase Difficulty

- Place a target progressively further outside the leg stump and turn the ball back to hit the stumps.

To Decrease Difficulty

- Place a target close to the stumps so you have to turn the ball only slightly to hit the stumps.

Success Check

- Grip the ball correctly, with the ball cupped between your first and second fingers, the base of your thumb and a bent third finger.

- Move in a straight line towards the target.
- Bring your arm over high.
- At the moment of release, straighten your third finger and rotate your wrist to impart more spin.
- Strike through with a fast arm to give the action snap.

Score Your Success

5 or 6 balls turn from leg to off = 5 points

3 or 4 balls turn from leg to off = 3 points

1 or 2 balls turn from leg to off = 1 point

Your Score ___

Spin Bowling Drill 3. *Googlies*

Using a red-and-white-halved ball, bowl six googlies. Make sure you can see only one colour as the ball goes towards the batsman.

To Increase Difficulty

- Place a target progressively further outside the off-stump and turn the ball back to hit the stumps.

To Decrease Difficulty

- Place a target down close to the stumps so you have to turn the ball only slightly to hit the stumps.

Success Check

- Grip the ball correctly, with the ball cupped between your first and second fingers, the base of your thumb and a bent third finger.

- Move in a straight line towards the target.
- Bring your arm over high and drop your front shoulder as you release the ball.
- At the moment of release, straighten your third finger and rotate your wrist so that the ball comes out over your fingers with the back of your hand facing the batsman.
- Strike through with a fast arm to give the action snap.

Score Your Success

5 or 6 balls turn from off to leg = 5 points

3 or 4 balls turn from off to leg = 3 points

1 or 2 balls turn from off to leg = 1 point

Your Score ___

Spin Bowling Drill 4. *Off-Spinners and Arm Ball*

Bowl six off-spinners, or left-arm spinners, to a batsman and put in one arm ball. Have the batsman attempt to hit the ball.

To Increase Difficulty

- Try to bowl progressively further outside off-stump and turn the ball back to hit the stumps, or get the ball to swing away further in the air if you are bowling an arm ball.

To Decrease Difficulty

- Try to bowl closer to the stumps so you have only to turn the ball slightly to hit them, or just swing the arm ball enough to get it just off the straight.

Success Check

- Grip the ball correctly, with your first two fingers spread along the seam.
- Make sure that your thumb is not impeding the spin.

- Take a short delivery stride and pivot your front foot as you bowl.
- Reinforce the spin from your fingers by turning your whole hand as you release the ball.
- At the completion of the action, your body should have turned 180 degrees so what was your bowling shoulder is now pointing at the target.
- Grip the ball for the arm ball (floater) with the seam upright and pointing in the direction you want the ball to swing; go right through with your action.

Score Your Success

5 or 6 balls behave as intended = 5 points

3 or 4 balls behave as intended = 3 points

1 or 2 balls behave as intended = 1 point

Your Score ___

Spin Bowling Drill 5. *Leg Breaks and Googly*

Bowl six leg breaks to a batsman and put in one googly. The batsman attempts to hit the ball.

To Increase Difficulty

- Try to pitch the ball progressively further outside the line of the stumps and turn the ball back to hit them.

To Decrease Difficulty

- Try to bowl closer to the stumps so you have only to turn the ball slightly to hit them.

Success Check

- Grip the ball correctly, with the ball cupped between your first and second fingers, the base of your thumb and a bent third finger.
- Make sure that you are moving in a straight line towards the target.

- Bring your arm over high.
- At the moment of release, straighten your third finger and rotate your wrist to impart more spin.
- Strike through with a fast arm to give the action snap.
- For the googly, drop your front shoulder a little, if necessary, and release the ball with the back of your bowling hand facing the batsman.

Score Your Success

5 or 6 balls behave as intended = 5 points

3 or 4 balls behave as intended = 3 points

1 or 2 balls behave as intended = 1 point

Your Score ___

SUCCESS SUMMARY OF SPIN BOWLING

Successful spin bowling is all about control and deception. The more you can turn the ball, the more successful you are likely to be. You only have to turn it a few inches to beat the bat. On some pitches, you will not be able to turn the ball as much as on others, but then you have the option of beating the batsman with clever flight.

The grip is all important to ensure you are able to turn the ball. Make sure you use the right grip for whatever style of spin bowler you are. If you are bowling off-spin, or left-arm orthodox, pivot on your front leg and make sure you do not take too long a delivery stride. If you bowl leg spin, remember to move your body directly towards the target and bowl with a snap in your action.

Before moving on to step 4, Basic Batting, evaluate how you did on the spin bowling drills in this step. Tally your scores to determine how well you have mastered the skill of spin bowling. If you scored at least 15 points, you are ready to move on to step 4. If you did not score at least 15 points, practice the drills again until you raise your scores before moving on to step 4.

Spin Bowling Drills

1. Off-Break Bowling   ___ out of 5

2. Leg-Break Bowling   ___ out of 5

3. Googlies   ___ out of 5

4. Off-Spinners and Arm Ball   ___ out of 5

5. Leg Breaks and Googly   ___ out of 5

Total   ___ *out of 25*

Now that you have dealt with bowling, either spin or pace, it is time to move on to batting. Even the best bowler in the world has to bat, and it is a good idea to become as proficient a batsman as possible. Like all other aspects of the game, there are some simple basics to be learned. Master those, and you will be scoring hundreds. Even if you consider yourself to be primarily a bowler, it is very useful to be able to contribute a few runs to the team's total. When it comes to a selection between two bowlers, the one who can bat usually gets the last place in the side.

Basic Batting

It is often said that cricket is a batsman's game. Perhaps it is the bowlers who say that, because they suspect that no sooner do they take the upper hand than the administrators help the batsmen restore their star status. In truth, the administrators are usually trying to re-establish parity because cricket is nothing without a fine balance between bat and ball. If batsmen were allowed to hold sway unchallenged, runs would be easy to come by, and the game as a whole would be devalued.

The object of batting is to score runs. There are times when the conservation of wickets is the prime objective because of the game situation. It is rare, even in the most ferocious fight for survival, that some runs are not scored. Runs are a batsman's oxygen, and unless he can make the occasional sortie to the other end or pick up the odd boundary, he will suffocate. This is the great dilemma of batting. There is a need for runs, but trying to score them more quickly than the bowling allows means taking risks. That, in turn, increases the likelihood of dismissal, and there has never been a batsman who has scored runs while sitting in the pavilion ruing the fall of his wicket.

Batsmen go to the middle with the intention of scoring runs—without runs on the board,

no side can expect to win. However, the game situation dictates how soon the incoming batsman is prepared to take risks. If there is plenty of time available, he can get used to the conditions, examine the bowling and gradually ease himself into his innings as his confidence grows with time at the crease. Conversely, towards the end of a limited-overs match, he might have to dispense with caution and go after the bowling from the very first ball.

As in every aspect of the game, the best players are those who do the simple things better than others. This is particularly true of batting. Without proper mastery of the basics, a batsman is unlikely to have the choice whether he tries to stay in or goes for runs. Any half-decent bowler will solve the batsman's problems by dismissing him. However, all the best batsmen attend to the basic principles, and only a genius can afford to flout them and still score consistently.

So what are these unforgiving principles, or the golden rules of batting? They are not complicated in themselves, but their application can be. Like so much in cricket, the key to successful batting is in your head. Before you even face a ball, you can give yourself a decent chance of playing well by getting your head in the right place and the correct position.

STANCE

Always take a guard when you get to the crease. The common guards are middle stump, middle and leg stump and leg stump (figure 4.1, a-c). The stumps are important because you hold your bat in front of them and ask the umpire for your guard. If you ask for middle stump, the umpire will tell you where that is on the popping crease.

Comply with his instructions and move the bat along the crease until it is right in front of middle stump. When it is, make a mark on the crease (figure 4.2) and prepare to face every ball from that position. The same applies to leg stump. Middle and leg stump refers to a position directly between the middle stump and the leg stump.

Figure 4.1   Common Guards

MIDDLE STUMP

1. Hold bat with its edge towards umpire
2. Shift toe of bat until it is straight in front of middle stump
3. Make a mark on the crease

a

MIDDLE AND LEG STUMP

1. Hold bat with its face towards the umpire
2. Shift toe of bat until it covers middle and leg stumps
3. Make a mark on the crease

b

50

LEG STUMP

1. Hold bat with its edge towards the umpire
2. Shift toe of bat until it is straight in front of leg stump
3. Make a mark on the crease

c

Figure 4.2 Mark on the crease.

Ask some batsmen why they take a particular guard, and they have little idea. Although they may offer some sort of idea, it seldom makes any sense. The suggestion that they take a leg-stump guard because they prefer playing on the off side is scarcely valid unless the bowler is prepared to co-operate by bowling as the batsman wants.

The reason for taking any guard is to ensure that your head is directly in front of the stumps. If you are tall and bend over a long way in your stance, you will need a leg-stump guard; otherwise, your head will be outside off-stump as you settle into your stance. Even if you are tall, if you stand upright in your stance, you might want to take middle so that your head is directly in front of the stumps. There is a good reason for this. The wicket is 9 inches (23 cm) wide, about the same size as a human head. Therefore, if your nose is in line with middle stump, and you keep your head still, you know that any ball passing wide of your right ear will miss off-stump; any ball wide of your left ear will pass by leg stump. If the ball is in line with your head, you had better get a bat on it to keep it out of the wicket.

Misstep
You don't know where the stumps are behind you.

Correction
Check your guard so that you know the stumps are always directly behind your head.

To make the best judgement about the line of the ball, keep your eyes as nearly parallel with the ground as possible. When you want to stare at something intently, you hold your head and eyes level; you don't cock your head to one side. Many batsmen cock their heads to one side and still try to watch a cricket ball intently. If you start like that, you will usually fall away with your head towards the off side. This means you are likely to bring the bat across the line of the ball from leg to off, reducing your chances of making good contact. Or if you bring your head up from that leaning stance, your eyes will need to adjust while the ball is on its way. That is not giving you the best chance to focus on the ball. By ensuring that your head is over middle stump with your eyes parallel to the ground, you will avoid these simple errors.

Misstep
You topple over towards the off side.

Correction
Stand more upright; make sure your eyes are level and not at an angle as you prepare to face the bowling.

The rest of your body is important as well. Your feet should be comfortably apart, with knees slightly flexed (figure 4.3, *a* and *b*), so that you are balanced and able to move backwards or forwards as the delivery demands. You should be side-on to the bowler because it will be easier to play straight. All you have to do is pick the bat up straight and let it come down straight again to keep your bat on the line of the ball for as long as possible. This gives you the best chance of making contact. If you swish across the line, your bat path and the line of the ball will coincide for no more than a split second. If you are extremely talented and well co-ordinated, you may still be able to hit the ball in those circumstances. But you are more likely to make contact if the path of your bat and the line of the ball are the same, although travelling in opposite directions. If you are a little early or a little late, you will not hit the ball as you intend, but you will still hit it.

Figure 4.3   **Stance**

FRONT VIEW

1. Stand side-on to the bowler
2. Place feet comfortably apart and parallel to crease
3. Keep knees slightly flexed
4. Hold head upright
5. Keep eyes parallel to ground

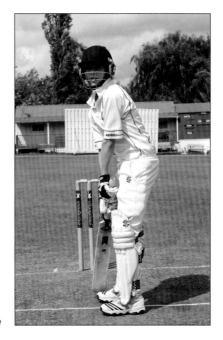

a

SIDE VIEW

1. Stand side-on
2. Place feet comfortably apart and parallel to crease
3. Keep knees slightly flexed
4. Hold head upright
5. Keep eyes parallel to ground

b

GRIP

It also is important to hold the bat properly. When Tiger Woods gets ready to tee up, the first thing he does is look at where he wants to hit the ball, even before he checks his grip. That golf ball is not going anywhere until Woods hits it; you, however, are going to have a cricket ball coming towards you at up to 90 miles (145 km) per hour. If it is worth it to Woods to check his grip, that should make sense for you, too. Get into the habit of checking your grip before every ball to give yourself the best chance to hit it.

Hold your hands close together on the handle (figure 4.4). This enables your hands to work together, rather than having one dominate the other. It is one of the quirks of cricket that the dominant, and therefore strongest, hand is in the position where it can hinder rather than help correct stroke play. A right-handed batsman will grip the bat with his left hand near the top of the handle and his right hand just below it; the top hand will control the shots. If the bottom, or right, hand takes over, the batsman will hit across the line as his right hand pushes through and his head falls over. He will be in no position to play.

Your grip can help prevent this from happening. Put your top hand on the bat so the point of the V formed by your thumb and forefinger is in line with a point halfway between the middle of the splice and the outside edge of the bat. The back of your left hand should face mid-off. Then put your right hand just below the left with

Figure 4.4 Hands are close together on the handle with the top hand near the top of the handle. The Vs formed by the thumb and forefinger on both hands are in line and midway between the middle of the splice and the outside edge.

the V of that hand in line with that of the top hand. If you get the grip right, the face of the bat will come down at a right angle to the line of the ball, giving you the best possible chance of hitting it cleanly.

Misstep
You hit every ball towards the leg side.

Correction
Your grip is faulty. Make sure your grip on the bat is correct and that you are not letting your bottom hand take over.

BACKLIFT

Cricketers talk of bringing the bat down on the ball, but first you need to pick up the bat. It can be taken up towards third man and still come down straight, but it is much simpler to avoid the need for adjustment by picking it up straight in the first place. That means the bat will go back over middle stump (you know where that is—it is directly behind your nose!) with your top hand pushing it back and up rather than your bottom hand pulling it up (figure 4.5, *a* and *b*).

Figure 4.5   Backlift

FRONT VIEW

1. Top hand pushes bat straight back and up
2. Toe of bat is higher than hands
3. Hands are above waist

a

SIDE VIEW

1. Top hand pushes bat straight back and up
2. Toe of bat is higher than hands
3. Hands are above waist

b

Misstep
You get no power in your shots.
Correction
You need to employ a higher backlift and make sure that it is straight back.

To play down on the ball, get the toe of the bat above your hands and your hands above your waist. Your forearm will be parallel to the ground if you have picked up the bat properly. Too many batsmen think they are picking up the bat high enough if they merely cock their wrists in their stance. They are not. If the ball bounces, they have to bring their hands up, and that invariably makes them hit the ball in the air. Make sure you pick up the bat early. It takes time to lift your bat high. It is no use starting your backlift when the ball is already on its way. Pick the bat up when the bowler is in his delivery stride so that no matter how quick his delivery is, all you have to do is bring the bat straight down.

JUDGING THE LINE OF THE BALL

You know how to judge the line of the ball because your head is in line with the stumps. You will pick up this line early and get an idea of length if you watch the ball all the way from the bowler's hand. As you took guard, the umpire told you where the ball would be coming from by announcing, 'Right arm over' or whatever. Focus on the point from where the ball is to be released. If you can see how the bowler is holding the ball, you might get an idea of what he is going to bowl; however, you will not be able to keep watching the ball as the bowler's hand sweeps over in his action. Therefore, focus on that small area from where you know the ball is going to come. That way, you will see the ball much earlier than if you look in the general direction of the bowler and try to pick up the ball after it has left his hand.

Batting can be made more complicated than it should be. These basic routines of standing properly; using a correct grip; and then lifting the bat up straight, high and early all happen before the ball reaches you. All players can perform these basics just as well as a Test batsman. Without perfecting them, though, you will not give yourself the best chance of dealing with the ball when it does arrive.

Basic Batting Drill 1. *Grip Check*

Take hold of the bat six times while a partner checks your grip. A coach, experienced player or a friend from the team can evaluate your grip. If a partner is unavailable, look in a mirror to check that your grip, stance and backlift conform to the photographs in this step.

Success Check

- Grip the bat with the Vs in line midway between the splice and the outside edge.

- Check whether your hands are close together on the bat handle.

Score Your Success

6 correct grips = 5 points

3 to 5 correct grips = 1 point

1 or 2 correct grips = 0 points

Your Score ___

Basic Batting Drill 2. *Stance Check*

Take your stance as if you are about to face a ball and have a partner check you. Get into your stance six times.

To Increase Difficulty

- Have your partner check that you maintain this position as a bowler comes in to deliver a real ball.

Success Check

- Stand side-on, feet comfortably apart.

- Flex your knees.
- Keep your eyes level and parallel to the ground.

Score Your Success

6 correct stances = 5 points

3 to 5 correct stances = 1 point

1 or 2 correct stances = 0 points

Your Score ___

Basic Batting Drill 3.   *Backlift Check*

Have your partner check your backlift; swing the bat back six times.

To Increase Difficulty

- Have your partner check whether you pick the bat up and bring it down straight when a bowler delivers a real ball to you.

Success Check

- With your top hand in control, lift the bat straight behind you over the middle stump.
- With your front forearm parallel to the ground, get the toe of the bat above your hands and your hands above your waist.

- Bring the bat down straight as if playing a forward defensive stroke (see step 5).

Score Your Success

6 correct backlifts = 5 points

3 to 5 correct backlifts = 1 point

1 or 2 correct backlifts = 0 points

Your Score ____

Basic Batting Drill 4.   *Complete Position Check*

Have your partner check your complete set-up, including grip, stance and backlift. Get into position and face a bowler who bowls six balls at you.

To Increase Difficulty

- Face a very good bowler who causes you to hurry.

To Decrease Difficulty

- Have a bowler simply lob balls towards you rather than bowl properly.

Success Check

- Ensure the grip is correct.

- Have your partner check your stance.
- Check that your backlift is high and straight, and that the bat comes straight down.
- Make sure you do not move your feet until you have seen the length and line of the ball.

Score Your Success

6 balls with correct set-up = 5 points

3 to 5 balls with correct set-up = 3 points

1 or 2 balls with correct set-up = 1 point

Your Score ____

SUCCESS SUMMARY OF BASIC BATTING

Compared to other steps in this book, basic batting might not appear to be a very exciting step. However, just as you cannot hope to be a decent bowler until you have mastered the basics, you cannot become a proficient batsman until you are in full command of the basic rules of batting.

Before facing each ball, check your grip in order to use the full face of the bat to play the ball. Make sure you are standing correctly. Get ready to lift your bat straight back over middle stump with your hands high. It all sounds very simple—and it is—but faults in meeting these basic requirements account for so much of what goes wrong in cricket. Make sure you do not succumb to basic errors. Move on to score hundreds of runs.

Before moving on to step 5, Defensive Batting, evaluate how you did on the basic batting drills in this step. Tally your scores to determine how well you have mastered the elements of basic batting. A total of 20 points is possible. If you scored 18 points, you are ready to move on to step 5. If you did not score 18 points, practice the drills again until you raise your scores before moving on to step 5.

Basic Batting Drills

1. Grip Check	___ out of 5
2. Stance Check	___ out of 5
3. Backlift Check	___ out of 5
4. Complete Position Check	___ out of 5
Total	___ *out of 20*

Now that your set-up is correct, you are ready to move on to step 5, Defensive Batting. You can have the best set-up the game has ever seen, but unless you hit the ball, you are not going to get very far as a batsman. The next step applies what you have learnt in this step to make sure you are able to defend your wicket. And when you can do that confidently, you can start to think about scoring runs.

Defensive Batting

There are two principal types of stroke played in cricket. Supposedly, batsmen refer to them as the 'get past that' stroke and the 'fetch that' stroke. The 'get past that' stroke is a defensive stroke that prevents the ball from getting through. The 'fetch that' stroke is an attacking stroke that sends the ball racing towards the boundary so one of the fielders has to go to get it. Unless you are able to describe a defensive stroke with conviction by imagining that you are saying, 'Get past that' to the bowler, you are unlikely to survive long enough at the crease to say, 'Fetch that' very often. Unless you are really trying to wind up the bowler, say these phrases to yourself, rather than out loud.

A batsman should intend to score off every ball, although the bowler can force him to change his mind. If a ball is likely to get you out if you attack it, you must be prepared to accept the bowler's superiority for that delivery. Have patience. Nothing is worse than getting out and then watching the next batsman dispatch a succession of long hops and half volleys. Had you treated the ball that dismissed you with a little more respect, you could have been the one taking advantage of those wayward deliveries.

Within the 'get past that' category, there are only two possibilities. You can move either backwards or forwards to counter a ball that is directed at the stumps, and then offer the broadest of bats to keep the ball out. This is an important rule to keep in mind. You should never play a defensive shot to a ball that is not going to hit the stumps. When you play defensively, you are not trying to score runs. Instead of the bat hitting the ball, you are allowing the ball to hit the bat. If you are not trying to score runs, why play a ball that is not threatening the wicket? If it is wide of the stumps, it is not going to bowl you. You cannot be LBW, but you might offer a catch by playing this otherwise harmless delivery.

This means that there is another possibility: the leave. When you decide that the percentages of playing a particular ball are not in your favour, let it go. Think of this as a positive action because you made a conscious decision to leave the ball alone. But make sure your bat and gloves are well out of the way. There are plenty of instances of a batsman trying to leave a ball only to have it take an edge and deflect onto the stumps. It is just as infuriating to draw away from a bouncing delivery and have it flick a glove, offering a simple catch. Like all shots, the leave needs practice.

FORWARD DEFENSIVE

Although often considered the most boring stroke in cricket, the forward defensive is also the most important. It is played to a good-length ball that is going to hit the stumps, and this is exactly the ball that the bowler tries to deliver every time. The dangers inherent in the forward defensive stroke illustrate why it is so important to have sound technique.

As with every other cricket shot, you need a high backlift (figure 5.1a) to play a forward defensive effectively. You might ask why this is, when all you are going to do is put your bat in the way and allow the ball to hit it. The answer is that before the bowler lets go of the ball, you intend to score runs if possible; therefore, it is important to get your hands and bat high in readiness for an attacking stroke. This movement should take place even before you can judge the line and length of the ball. And it carries another advantage: you want to bring your bat down onto the ball. Failure to get your hands high in the backlift can result in your hitting the ball into the air.

Figure 5.1	Forward Defensive Stroke

HIGH BACKLIFT

1. Top hand pushes bat straight back and up
2. Toe of bat is higher than hands
3. Hands are above waist

a

HEAD AND FRONT SHOULDER MOVEMENT

1. Lead with head and front shoulder towards pitch of the ball

b

EXECUTION, FRONT VIEW

1. Head in line with where ball pitched
2. Top hand in control
3. Bat brought down in angled position
4. Ball contacted slightly ahead of front pad

c

EXECUTION, SIDE VIEW

1. Weight on front foot
2. Front knee bent
3. Head over front knee
4. Back foot parallel to crease
5. Back heel raised slightly
6. Back leg straight

d

Misstep
You keep getting bowled by balls you think you have covered.

Correction
You are most likely bringing the bat down across the line. This may be because you are not lifting the bat straight up, or you are toppling to the off side and allowing your bottom hand to take over.

Once you have decided that the ball is threatening the stumps and is of a good length—not full enough to drive but not short enough for you to move backwards—the next movement is with your head and front shoulder (figure 5.1*b*). Generations of batsmen were taught to get their front feet to the pitch of the ball. What nonsense! This led to them plunging forward, often too early, so that not only would they find their feet in the wrong place, but their heads would not be in the correct position either.

There is a very good illustration for this point. If you are walking along the street and see money on the ground, you would not put your foot alongside it as you picked it up. What you would do is lead with your head towards the money, and almost magically, your foot would move to the right place as you bent down to pick it up.

In fact, this is not magic at all. If your foot did not take up that position, you would fall over as you leaned forward. As you pick up the money, your foot automatically moves to an ideal position for the forward defensive stroke.

If you concentrate on leading out towards the ball with your head, your foot will follow correctly. It will be in the right place, straight under your head and 45 degrees to the line of the ball. If your foot points straight down the pitch, it is a sure sign that you have moved it first and need to get it out of the way to allow the bat to come through. It also means that you do not have a firm base and are likely to topple over. With your foot in the 45-degree position, you will be balanced throughout the shot. This should happen naturally if you concentrate on getting the head movement right.

Misstep
Your pad gets in the way when you are playing the forward defensive.

Correction
You have moved your front leg before assessing the line of the ball.

With your weight balanced over a bent front knee and your back heel raised off the ground but with that foot parallel to the crease, you are in a good position to play the ball (figure 5.1*c*). If you allow your back foot to pivot so that the top rather than the inner side is in contact with the ground, your back leg is likely to collapse at the knee, prompting your body to fall backwards, and you will hit across the line. If you have assumed a good position, you will be able to bring the angled bat down on the ball with your top hand in control and your bottom hand relaxed into a thumb and forefinger grip (figure 5.1*d*).

The ball should hit the middle of the bat (figure 5.2). There is a danger of playing this shot too low. If you do, and the ball bounces, there is every chance that it will take the corner of the bat or your glove and offer a catch. To avoid giving a catch off the inside edge, play with the bat just in advance of your front leg. This should ensure that inside edges pass harmlessly down past the leg stump. If you ram your bat against

that front leg, an edge may pop up to waiting fielders, and you would have no room to adjust to a late swinging delivery.

Figure 5.2 The ball hits the middle of the bat on a forward defensive stroke.

Misstep
When playing forward defensively, you pop up catches in front of the wicket.

Correction
Make sure the bat is angled down; allow the ball to come to the bat rather than pushing out at it.

FORWARD DEFENSIVE DRILLS

In order to concentrate on the techniques involved, it is a good idea to run through all the batting drills using a tennis ball on a hard surface, such as in a sports hall or at a playground, unless stated otherwise. As you progress, you can put on full protective equipment and face a cricket ball in a suitable area, such as in a practice net or on the pitch itself.

Forward Defensive Drill 1. *Playing Forward Defensive Strokes*

Work with a partner or coach, or simply stand in front of a mirror, and play six forward defensive strokes to imaginary balls.

Success Check

- Make sure your set-up is correct and use a high backlift.
- Lead with your head towards the imaginary ball.
- Bring the bat down with the top hand in control and the bottom hand relaxed into a thumb and forefinger grip.

- At the completion of the shot, make sure your bat is angled down.

Score Your Success

5 or 6 correct forward defensive shots = 5 points

3 or 4 correct forward defensive shots = 3 points

1 or 2 correct forward defensive shots = 1 point

Your Score ___

Forward Defensive Drill 2. *Forward Defensive Strokes With Rotation*

Work in threes: one player bats; one feeds straight, good-length balls; and the third player acts as wicket-keeper. You can involve additional fielders if available. The batsman plays a forward defensive stroke to the balls. Once the batsman has faced six balls, the players change around so that everybody gets a chance to bat, feed and keep wicket.

To Increase Difficulty

- Increase the speed of the service of the ball.
- Place fielders all around the bat who are ready to catch anything that goes off the bat in the air.

To Decrease Difficulty

- Decrease the speed of the service of the ball.
- If fielders are used, place them farther away from the bat.

Success Check

- Make sure your set-up is correct and use a high backlift.
- When you have judged the line and length of the ball, lead with your head towards the ball.
- Bring the bat down on the ball with the top hand in control and the bottom hand relaxed into a thumb and forefinger grip.
- At the completion of the shot, make sure the ball drops straight down in front of you off the downward-angled bat.

Score Your Success

5 or 6 safe forward defensive shots = 5 points

3 or 4 safe forward defensive shots = 3 points

1 or 2 safe forward defensive shots = 1 point

Your Score ___

Forward Defensive Drill 3. *Wicket or Not?*

Play six forward defensive strokes against a ball served to you. Judge whether the ball is going to hit the wicket or not. Play a stroke only if you think the ball would go on to hit the stumps. If not, leave it. Have a colleague watch and keep score.

To Increase Difficulty

- Increase the speed of the service of the ball.
- Place fielders all around the bat who are ready to catch anything that goes off the bat in the air.

To Decrease Difficulty

- Decrease the speed of the service of the ball.
- If fielders are used, place them farther away from the bat.

Success Check

- Make sure your set-up is correct and use a high backlift.

- When you have judged the line and length of the ball, lead with your head towards the ball.
- Bring the bat down on the ball with the top hand in control and the bottom hand relaxed into a thumb and forefinger grip.
- At the completion of the shot, make sure the ball drops straight down in front of you off the downward-angled bat.

Score Your Success

5 or 6 correct judgements as to when to play a forward defensive shot = 5 points

3 or 4 correct judgements as to when to play a forward defensive shot = 3 points

1 or 2 correct judgements as to when to play a forward defensive shot = 1 point

Your Score ___

Forward Defensive Drill 4. *Practice Against Bowler*

Play against a bowler in a practice situation. Play forward defensive strokes against six balls when the delivery warrants it. Again, get a colleague to observe whether your judgement is sound and to keep score.

To Increase Difficulty

- Face a better bowler who tests your technique more and bring in some close fielders looking for a catch.

To Decrease Difficulty

- Face a bowler who does not present such a stern test and dispense with fielders.

Success Check

- Make sure your set-up is correct and use a high backlift.
- When you have judged the line and length of the ball, lead with your head towards the ball.

- Bring the bat down on the ball with the top hand in control and the bottom hand relaxed into a thumb and forefinger grip.
- At the completion of the shot, make sure the ball drops straight down in front of you off the downward-angled bat.

Score Your Success

5 or 6 correct playing of forward defensive shots = 5 points

3 or 4 correct playing of forward defensive shots = 3 points

1 or 2 correct playing of forward defensive shots = 1 point

Your Score ___

BACKWARD DEFENSIVE

If the ball is just short of a length and threatening the wicket, you need to move backwards. Given the tendency to plunge onto the front foot, players seem to find moving backwards more difficult than moving forwards. But if you learn to go back towards the stumps in the correct fashion, batting should become a far easier experience.

Fast bowlers would give their eye teeth for an extra yard of pace. However when you use the full depth of the crease to go backwards, you effectively add an extra yard to the length of the pitch, thereby reducing the bowler's pace. Once you have moved in the correct manner, you need to present the bowler with another challenge to 'get past that'.

When you moved forwards to play defensively, the first thing you moved was your head. Almost the same thing applies to moving backwards. Get your head in line with the ball, and your feet will automatically go to the right place to maintain balance. The slight difference from the forward defensive, apart from the direction of movement, is that you want your weight to be slightly forward. Coaches talk about moving backwards with your head left behind so that you do not lean back while playing the shot. Although your head determines the line, your back foot, moving at the same time as your head, enables you to get into line and to get back far enough.

Because you are only going to defend if the ball is heading for the stumps, you should not need to go very far in a lateral direction. One of the major faults of batsmen who move backwards, especially against quicker bowlers, is a tendency to back away to leg. That spells trouble. The batsman exposes his stumps to the full view of the bowler and is in no position to defend them. Courage is required of a batsman—and courage is not shown if you back away.

Once you have moved your back foot backwards to land parallel with the crease, enabling your head to be over the line of the ball, bring your front foot alongside the back one. This helps you maintain a side-on position rather than, as too often happens, playing the backward defensive shot with your chest facing the bowler. Fast bowlers are aggressive by nature, and you do not want to present them with a larger target than necessary! Furthermore, if you have moved backwards with your head over the line of the ball and your body just inside that line, it will be easier for you to execute the stroke.

Misstep

When you are playing back defensively, you have to bring your bat down and around your body to play the ball.

Correction

Check the position of your toes. You have likely opened up as you went backwards so that your toes are pointing back down the pitch rather than being parallel to the popping crease.

Once you have lifted your bat high and early and have taken up the prescribed position, all you need to do is bring your bat straight down for the ball to hit it (figure 5.3a). If you have gone too far over to the off side or have been squared up as you went back with your toes pointing towards the bowler, you will not be able to do this. Instead, you will have to make an adjustment by either getting the bat around your body or straightening the bat as it comes down to get it in line. Neither conforms to the requirement to keep batting simple.

Misstep

When you move backwards, you find that you are playing defensively away from your body.

Correction

You are either moving straight back rather than back and across, or you are defending balls that are too wide.

As with all back-foot shots, move into position for the backward defensive and then play the ball. The speed of the ball and your movement determine how much time you have between moving and playing, but this sequence should be what you strive for. You need a high backlift to ensure that you bring your hands down onto the ball. Ensure that your top hand is control, with your bottom hand relaxed into a thumb and forefinger grip and the bat angled down at impact (figure 5.3b).

Misstep

You find yourself playing the ball up rather than keeping it down.

Correction

As you move backwards, keep your head forward rather than leaning back, and do not let your bottom hand push through.

Figure 5.3　　Backward Defensive Stroke

EXECUTION, FRONT VIEW

1. Have top hand in control
2. Bring bat down at an angle
3. Maintain perfect balance
4. Play stroke

a

EXECUTION, SIDE VIEW

1. Play ball out in front of your head
2. Get head behind line of ball
3. Play off firm base

b

Remember that both defensive shots are designed solely to conserve your wicket. But it is not enough to keep the ball out of the stumps if you make a slight error that results in a catch. It is important to ensure you play defensive strokes with what are called soft hands. This means that you should not thrust the bat at the ball with a firm grip but allow the ball to come to you and meet it with your bottom hand relaxed. Then, should the ball find the edge, the chances are that it will not carry to waiting fielders. You will have achieved what you wanted: survival to face the next delivery that might easily be put away for four.

Backward Defensive Drill 1. *Playing Backward Defensive Strokes*

Work with a partner or coach, or simply stand in front of a mirror, and play six backward defensive strokes to imaginary balls.

Success Check

- Make sure your set-up is correct and use a high backlift.
- Move backwards far enough to get your head in line with the imaginary ball.
- Bring the bat down with your top hand in control and your bottom hand relaxed into a thumb and forefinger grip.

- Make sure your bat is angled down at the completion of the shot.

Score Your Success

5 or 6 correct backward defensive shots = 5 points

3 or 4 correct backward defensive shots = 3 points

1 or 2 correct backward defensive shots = 1 point

Your Score ____

Backward Defensive Drill 2. *Backward Defensive Strokes With Rotation*

Work in threes: one player bats; one feeds straight balls just short of a length; and the third player acts as wicket-keeper. You can involve additional fielders if available. The batsman plays a backward defensive to any ball that warrants it. Once the batsman has faced six balls, the players change around so that everybody gets a chance to bat, feed and keep wicket.

To Increase Difficulty

- Increase the speed of the service of the ball.
- Place fielders all around the bat who are ready to catch anything that goes off the bat into the air.

To Decrease Difficulty

- Decrease the speed of the service of the ball.
- If fielders are used, place them farther away from the bat.

Success Check

- Make sure your set-up is correct and use a high backlift.
- When you have judged the line and length of the ball, move backwards beside the line with your head left behind to keep your weight forward and stay side-on.
- Bring the bat down on the ball with your top hand in control and your bottom hand relaxed into a thumb and forefinger grip.
- At the completion of the shot, make sure the ball drops straight down in front of you off the downward-angled bat.

Score Your Success

5 or 6 safe backward defensive shots = 5 points

3 or 4 safe backward defensive shots = 3 points

1 or 2 safe backward defensive shots = 1 point

Your Score ____

Backward Defensive Drill 3. *Wicket or Not?*

Play six backward defensive strokes against a ball served to you. Judge whether the ball is going to hit the wicket and only play a stroke if you think the ball would go on to hit the stumps. If not, leave it. Ask a colleague to watch and keep score.

To Increase Difficulty

- Increase the speed of the service of the ball.
- Place fielders all around the bat who are ready to catch anything that goes off the bat into the air.

To Decrease Difficulty

- Decrease the speed of the service of the ball.
- If fielders are used, place them farther away from the bat.

Success Check

- Make sure your set-up is correct and use a high backlift.

- When you have judged the line and length of the ball, move backwards in the crease, remaining side-on so that you finish in a balanced position with your head over the line of the ball.
- Bring the bat down on the ball with your top hand in control and your bottom hand relaxed into a thumb and forefinger grip.
- At the completion of the shot, make sure the ball drops straight down in front of you off the downward-angled bat.

Score Your Success

5 or 6 correct judgements as to when to play a backward defensive shot = 5 points

3 or 4 correct judgements as to when to play a backward defensive shot = 3 points

1 or 2 correct judgements as to when to play a backward defensive shot = 1 point

Your Score ___

Backward Defensive Drill 4. *Practice Against Bowler*

Play against a bowler in a practice situation. Play backward defensive strokes against six balls when the delivery warrants it. Again, ask a colleague to observe whether your judgement is sound and to keep score.

To Increase Difficulty

- Face a better bowler who tests your technique more and bring in some close fielders looking for a catch.

To Decrease Difficulty

- Face a bowler who does not present such a stern test and dispense with fielders.

Success Check

- Make sure your set-up is correct and use a high backlift.
- When you have judged the line and length of the ball, move backwards in the crease;

remain side-on so that you finish in a balanced position with your head over the line of the ball.
- Bring the bat down on the ball with your top hand in control and your bottom hand relaxed into a thumb and forefinger grip.
- At the completion of the shot, make sure the ball drops straight down in front of you off the downward-angled bat.

Score Your Success

5 or 6 correct backward defensive shots = 5 points

3 or 4 correct backward defensive shots = 3 points

1 or 2 correct backward defensive shots = 1 point

Your Score ___

Defensive Batting Drill. *Forward and Backward Defensive Strokes*

Play against a bowler in a practice situation. Play forward or backward defensive strokes against six balls when the delivery warrants it. Again, ask a colleague to observe whether your judgement is sound and to keep score.

To Increase Difficulty

- Face a better bowler who tests your technique more and bring in some close fielders looking for a catch.

To Decrease Difficulty

- Face a bowler who does not present such a stern test and dispense with fielders.

Success Check

- Make sure your set-up is correct and use a high backlift.
- When you have judged the line and length of the ball, if you are playing a backward defensive stroke, move backwards in the crease, remaining side-on; finish in a balanced position with your head over the line of the ball. If you are playing a forward defensive stroke, lead with your head towards the line of the ball.
- Bring the bat down on the ball with your top hand in control and your bottom hand relaxed into a thumb and forefinger grip.
- At the completion of the shot, make sure the ball drops straight down in front of you off the downward-angled bat.

Score Your Success

5 or 6 correct defensive shots = 5 points

3 or 4 correct defensive shots = 3 points

1 or 2 correct defensive shots = 1 point

Your Score ___

SUCCESS SUMMARY OF DEFENSIVE BATTING

In defensive batting, the first thing you must concentrate on is the line of the ball. If the ball is threatening the stumps, you need to defend by going either forwards or backwards, depending on the length of the ball. If it is a good length, go forwards; if it is short of a length, go backwards. Use a high backlift so you can bring your hands down onto the ball. Keep your top hand in control and relax the grip of the bottom hand as you allow the ball to hit the bat. Play the ball softly down straight in front of you.

Before moving on to step 6, Attacking Batting, evaluate how you did on the defensive batting drills in this step. Tally your scores to determine how well you have mastered the skill of defensive batting. If you scored 40 points, you are ready to move on to step 6. If you did not score 40 points, practice the drills again until you raise your scores and then move on to step 6.

Forward Defensive Drills

1.	Playing Forward Defensive Strokes	___ out of 5
2.	Forward Defensive Strokes With Rotation	___ out of 5
3.	Wicket or Not?	___ out of 5
4.	Practice Against Bowler	___ out of 5

Backward Defensive Drills

1.	Playing Backward Defensive Strokes	___ out of 5
2.	Backward Defensive Strokes With Rotation	___ out of 5
3.	Wicket or Not?	___ out of 5
4.	Practice Against Bowler	___ out of 5

Defensive Batting Drill

1.	Forward and Backward Defensive Strokes	___ out of 5
Total		___ **out of 45**

Once you have mastered the art of defensive batting, you are ready to move on to the exciting array of attacking strokes described in step 6, Attacking Batting. Unless you have a sound defence, though, you will not be at the wicket long enough to play those strokes. As you build your innings, you become accustomed to the conditions and the bowling. When you have, you will be ready to start inviting the fielders to 'fetch that'.

Attacking Batting

Nothing in cricket can match the elegance of a flowing cover drive or the excitement of a hook shot whistling to the boundary. This applies whether you are the batsman who has just executed the stroke or a spectator appreciating the finer points of the game. If you are the bowler who has just seen the effort of your delivery go to waste, you might have another viewpoint entirely. But the fact remains that attacking strokes bring the game to life. Sound defence is important, but if you are going to be a successful batsman, you must have a range of attacking shots.

That does not mean that you have to play them all. A batsman's individual style might restrict him from playing certain strokes with any degree of safety. For example, if you struggle to hook because you keep getting out to catches in the deep, it would be as well to duck or sway out of the way of short, lifting deliveries down the leg side. Attacking batting is all about percentages. If they are in your favour, go for the stroke; if the risk is too great, you would be better advised to exclude that particular stroke from your armoury. Of course, the game situation might demand that you take risks; in that case, you might have no alternative other than to attack the ball, but do not do so without having practiced the stroke you need.

Eliminating some shots from your repertoire might appear to be a negative way of playing cricket, but in reality it is not. It is a case of playing to your strengths rather than allowing deficiencies in your game to detract from your contribution. Some of the very best batsmen do not play all the strokes. If they are not proficient in playing the on-drive, for example, they might opt for a nudge into the leg side for a single. They may have sacrificed three runs, but they have kept the scoreboard moving and rotated the strike, which is preferable to losing a wicket.

A key to good attacking batting is the ability and the mindset to play every ball on its merit. Too many batsmen, particularly at the lower levels of the game, have a restricted range of strokes and a resulting preconception about which they will play. You cannot know where the ball is going to pitch until the bowler has delivered it, so wait until you have assessed the delivery before selecting your stroke. Bowlers are not keen to offer the type of ball that suits you. Good bowlers will work a batsman and bowl to his weaknesses, rather than to his strengths.

Just as bowlers assess batsmen and decide where to bowl at them, batsmen need to assess bowlers. If a bowler is not very good, a batsman knows he does not have to create scoring chances. He can simply wait for a bad ball and punish it because it will not be long before one comes along. Against better bowlers, however, it is necessary to manufacture a situation in which you can score runs because you will not receive as many bad balls. You can achieve this by moving down the wicket to turn a good-length ball into a half volley or by taking greater risks in order to unsettle the bowler and gain the upper hand.

Whatever strategy you adopt, it is absolutely vital that you attain a high level of technique when playing attacking strokes. Without that, what you envisaged as an on-drive might well end up as an ugly smear over mid-wicket, with all the associated risks. You might even miss the ball completely. Either way, you are not achieving the result you want, and you are reducing, rather than increasing, your chances of success.

When attacking the bowling, try not to hit the ball too hard. You tend to lose your balance if you do. Once that happens, you lose your shape, and the ball is likely to go in the air if you get any bat on it. That is one of the most common mistakes, most of which come down to not thinking properly about your batting. If you really smash the ball, and it goes along the ground, over the boundary rope, across the car park and into the road, you get four runs for your trouble. If you place the ball between fielders, and it has just enough power to go a couple of inches over the boundary, you still get four. Which do you think is the safer option?

FRONT-FOOT DRIVE

Whether straight or to the off, on or through the covers, drives are among the most glamorous shots in the game. They tend to be the most commonly played strokes, yet they probably cause more dismissals than any other when they are used inappropriately or played loosely. Choosing the right ball to drive is as important as how you play the stroke, so it is vital to establish exactly where a delivery comes within driving range.

A ball that is overpitched or of half-volley length can be dispatched to the boundary with a flowing bat. If the ball is straight, it should be driven straight back past the bowler (figure 6.1). If the ball is to the on side or the off, it should be played accordingly; if it is a little wider of the off-stump, the cover drive comes into play. All these strokes have common characteristics. Played correctly, they can bring a host of runs; however, they are not risk free, although most risks arise from poor technique or impatience in playing the stroke. You cannot decide before the ball is bowled that you are going to drive it or play any other stroke. Just because you like driving does not mean you should decide on the stroke before you have judged the length or the line.

Once you have determined that the ball has been overpitched and that you can safely drive it, lead with your head onto the line of the ball as with the forward defensive stroke. This time, however, instead of bringing the bat down to let the ball hit it, allow the bat to continue through the line to send the ball to the boundary (figure 6.2, a-d). Your top hand controls the stroke, bringing it down the line of the ball from that high, straight backlift so that, ideally, you make contact with the ball right under your head.

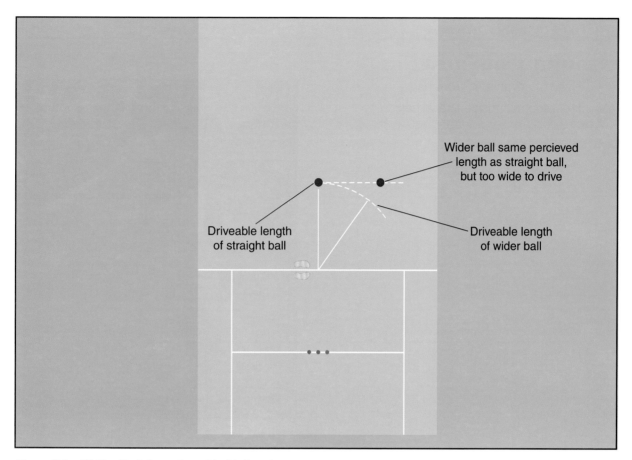

Figure 6.1 Width of ball determines drivable length.

Figure 6.2 **Front-Foot Drive**

EXECUTION, FRONT VIEW

1. From high backlift, lead with head and front shoulder towards the pitch of the ball
2. Keep top hand dominant as bat strikes ball

a

(continued)

Figure 6.2 *(continued)*

EXECUTION, SIDE VIEW

1. Head in advance of front pad
2. Front foot alongside line of ball

b

FULL FOLLOW-THROUGH, FRONT VIEW

1. Bat swings through line

c

FULL FOLLOW-THROUGH, SIDE VIEW

1. Finish with bat handle pointing in direction ball goes

d

Misstep
You hit the ball in the air every time you drive.

Correction
Make sure you get your head over the ball when driving; do not play the shot with your weight leaning back.

It is critical to keep your shape when driving. If you lose your shape, disaster can follow. If you try to hit the ball too hard, your back foot will pivot, and your back leg will collapse, forcing your body weight to fall back. A telltale sign of whether this has happened can be found in the follow-through. Review your follow-through to check whether your bat has travelled straight through the hitting zone.

Misstep
Every time you drive, the ball goes to mid-wicket or you miss it completely.

Correction
You are hitting across the line because you are trying to hit the ball too hard, your bottom hand is taking over as you allow your back leg to collapse or because of a combination of these factors.

There are two ways to follow through. Against quicker bowlers, you might want to use the pace on the ball to play with a checked follow-through, in which case you would not allow the bat to continue over your shoulder (figure 6.3, *a* and *b*). The bat stops, and your front elbow stays high, with the bat acting like an extension of your forearm. If you have swung it straight through the line of the ball, the blade will point where the ball has been dispatched. If you play with a full follow-through (see figure 6.2*c* and *d*), the handle of the bat will point at the ball. If neither the blade nor the handle is in the correct position, you have brought your bat across the line of the ball rather than through it.

Figure 6.3   Checked Follow-Through

CHECKED FOLLOW-THROUGH, FRONT VIEW

1. Bat looks like extension of forearm
2. Blade of bat points in direction ball goes

a

CHECKED FOLLOW-THROUGH, SIDE VIEW

1. Left elbow high

b

In order to hit cleanly through the line, you need to drive the ball along the line it pitched. If the ball is straight, drive it straight back past the bowler. If it is to the on side, drive through mid-on. If it is just outside off-stump, either side of mid-off is the target area. Some batsmen get into trouble trying to drive a ball too wide of off-stump through the covers. A cover drive is a beautiful shot to behold when executed well, but if it is played without proper judgement of length, it is fraught with problems.

If a ball on the line of middle stump pitches 3 feet (1 m) from the popping crease, a man of average height can easily get over it to drive it along the ground. However, if the ball pitches 18 inches (.5 m) outside off-stump but still 3 feet from the popping crease, the same batsman cannot get his head over it, for effectively it is several inches (cm) shorter. On a true pitch,

you might be able to drive it on the up, but the percentages are not necessarily in your favour. Furthermore, if you try to drive a ball too wide of the stumps, the bat is only on the line of the ball for a fraction of a second. It requires remarkable co-ordination to ensure that the bat crosses the line at exactly the same moment as the ball.

Sometimes, you actually will want to drive the ball in the air (figure 6.4), especially when using your feet to go down the pitch against a spinner. This is thrilling to watch, but it has to be undertaken with due care and only when you are confident that you can keep your shape throughout the stroke. When you do go down the pitch, you are under no obligation to drive over the top or even play an attacking stroke at all. If you have misjudged your sortie, you can still defend and survive to face the next ball.

Figure 6.4   Lofted Drive

EXECUTION

1. Maintain side-on shape but come up a little with torso in shot
2. Make contact slightly earlier
3. Use full follow-through

If you do go through with the stroke, make sure your head does not bob up and down but remains steady as you move. Remain side-on when you reach the pitch of the ball. In that position, swing the bat through the ball as with a static drive; as you make contact, raise your body up slightly and deliberately play the ball

upwards. Put enough into the stroke to ensure that it goes all the way for six or play it safely into a gap in the field. There is a lot of room in the air, but you will not be able to use it profitably unless you maintain a correct shape and have a technique that is up to the task.

Misstep
You get no power in your shot however hard you try to hit it.

Correction
Make sure you have a high backlift and do not try to hit the ball too hard. Instead, rely on timing.

Front-Foot Drive Drill 1. *Imaginary Front-Foot Drives*

Play front-foot drives against an imaginary ball with either a coach or experienced partner watching or in front of a mirror. Shape to play six balls, one each to leg, straight and to the off, with a full follow-through, and one of each with a checked follow-through.

Success Check

- Ensure you have a good set-up with a high backlift.
- Lead with your head towards the pitch of the imaginary ball.
- Keep your back foot parallel to the popping crease.

- Have your top hand in control as you bring the bat down into the hitting zone under your head.
- At the completion of the stroke, make sure either the blade of the bat or the handle points in the direction the ball has been hit.

Score Your Success

5 or 6 well-executed drives = 5 points

3 or 4 well-executed drives = 3 points

1 or 2 well-executed drives = 1 point

Your Score ___

Front-Foot Drive Drill 2. *Target Front-Foot Drives*

Mark a target with two cones. Exactly where the target is depends on the room available. In an average-size sports hall, for example, the target can be on the back wall. A feeder drops a ball. Attempt to drive it between the cones and along the ground. Hit six balls.

To Increase Difficulty

- Reduce the size of the target.
- Place fielders to guard the target.
- Have the feeder throw the ball towards you on the half volley or bobble it along the ground.

To Decrease Difficulty

- If you have difficulty hitting a moving ball, set the ball up on a tee and drive it off the tee.

Success Check

- Ensure you have a good set-up with a high backlift.

- Lead with your head towards the pitch of the ball.
- Keep your back foot parallel to the popping crease.
- Have your top hand in control as you bring the bat down to strike the ball under your head.
- At the completion of the stroke, make sure either the blade of the bat or the handle points in the direction the ball has been hit.

Score Your Success

5 or 6 balls driven along the ground between the target cones = 5 points

3 or 4 balls driven along the ground between the target cones = 3 points

1 or 2 balls driven along the ground between the target cones = 1 point

Your Score ___

Front-Foot Drive Drill 3. *Mix It Up*

Put on full protection and have a bowler deliver six balls for you to drive. Judge the line of the ball before deciding which of the three front-foot drives you are going to play. Use both a full and a checked follow-through. Play six front-foot drives aimed at a target of cones.

To Increase Difficulty

- Reduce the size of the target.
- Place fielders to guard the target.
- Get a more-challenging bowler to bowl at you.

To Decrease Difficulty

- Widen the target areas.
- Face a less-challenging bowler.

Success Check

- Ensure you have a good set-up with a high backlift.

- Lead with your head towards the pitch of the ball.
- Keep your back foot parallel to the popping crease.
- Have your top hand in control as you bring the bat down to strike the ball under your head.
- At the completion of the stroke, make sure either the blade of the bat or the handle points in the direction the ball has been hit.

Score Your Success

5 or 6 balls driven along the ground between the target cones = 5 points

3 or 4 balls driven along the ground between the target cones = 3 points

1 or 2 balls driven along the ground between the target cones = 1 point

Your Score ___

BACK-FOOT DRIVE

Just as the initial movements for front-foot drives are similar to the forward defensive stroke, so the back-foot drives begin with a movement allied to the backward defensive stroke. The shot, whether straight, to the on or to the off, is played to a ball that is short of a length and, critically, is not bouncing above stump height. If it bounces any higher, you will not be able to control the stroke.

 Misstep
When you try to force the ball off the back foot, the ball goes in the air.

Correction
You are probably trying to force a ball that is bouncing too high, and therefore you cannot get over the top of it.

A high backlift is important because low hands will prevent you from playing down to the ball. If you have a high, straight backlift, you will merely have to assess the line and move backwards with your head over the line and your body alongside it (figure 6.5, *a* and *b*). Make sure that when you move backwards, you keep your side-on position by bringing your front foot alongside the back one. Your top hand controls the stroke. If you have allowed the ball to come to you, your top hand brings the bat down on the line of the ball. Your bottom hand comes into play as you punch the ball away, finishing with the blade of the bat facing the point on the boundary where the ball is heading.

Figure 6.5 Back-Foot Drive

EXECUTION, FRONT VIEW

1. From high backlift, bring bat down
2. Keep top hand in control
3. Strike through line of ball under head
4. Bat handle looks like extension of front arm
5. Blade of bat points in direction ball goes

a

EXECUTION, SIDE VIEW

1. Move back foot backwards to get head in line
2. Draw feet alongside each other
3. Remain side-on
4. Maintain firm base
5. Left elbow held high

b

Misstep

When you attempt the shot, the ball tends to go in the air to the slips.

Correction

You are not getting across as well as going backwards; as a result, you are wafting at the ball rather than getting behind it.

Because you have a small margin for error in moving into a balanced position, don't attempt to hit the ball too hard. If you lose your balance, you are likely to lose your wicket, too. By playing this controlled stroke you will not need a flourishing follow-through. Be content with a checked swing of the bat, with your front elbow the highest part of your body when you complete the stroke.

This forcing shot can be played into the same areas as the front-foot drive: straight, to the on and off sides and even through the covers. However, the same restrictions apply. Do not try to play it too wide of the stumps, especially outside the off-stump, because you will risk hitting across the line. To prevent this from happening, move backwards and across. Make sure you know where your wicket is to stop yourself from chasing balls that are too wide.

Misstep

You get no power in your shot however hard you try to hit it.

Correction

For this shot, you need to time the ball rather than belt it. You need a high backlift to come down on the ball, and it is vital that you retain your balance.

Back-Foot Drive Drill 1. *Imaginary Back-Foot Drives*

Play back-foot drives against an imaginary ball with either a coach or experienced partner watching or in front of a mirror. Shape to play six balls, one each to leg, straight and to the off, with a checked follow-through.

Success Check

- Ensure you have a good set-up with a high backlift.
- Lead with your head towards the pitch of the imaginary ball.
- Keep your back foot parallel to the popping crease.

- Have your top hand in control as you bring the bat down into the hitting zone under your head.
- At the completion of the stroke, make sure either the blade of the bat or the handle points in the direction the ball has been hit.

Score Your Success

5 or 6 well-executed drives = 5 points

3 or 4 well-executed drives = 3 points

1 or 2 well-executed drives = 1 point

Your Score ___

Back-Foot Drive Drill 2.   *Target Back-Foot Drives*

Mark a target with two cones. Exactly where the target is depends on the room available. In an average-size sports hall, for example, the target can be on the back wall. A feeder serves the ball without allowing it to bounce above stump height. Attempt to drive the ball between the cones and along the ground. Hit six balls.

To Increase Difficulty

- Reduce the size of the target.
- Place fielders to guard the target.

To Decrease Difficulty

- If you have difficulty hitting a moving ball, set the ball up on a tall tee and drive it off the tee.

Success Check

- Ensure you have a good set-up with a high backlift.

- Move backwards to get into line while maintaining a side-on position and leaving your head behind.
- Have your top hand in control as you bring the bat down to strike the ball close to your body.
- At the completion of the stroke, make sure the blade of the bat points in the direction the ball has been hit, with the bat as an extension of your forearm.

Score Your Success

5 or 6 balls driven along the ground between the target cones = 5 points

3 or 4 balls driven along the ground between the target cones = 3 points

1 or 2 balls driven along the ground between the target cones = 1 point

Your Score ___

Back-Foot Drive Drill 3.   *Mix It Up*

Put on full protection and have a bowler deliver six balls for you to drive. Judge the line of the ball before deciding which of the three back-foot drives you are going to play. Play six back-foot drives aimed at a target of cones.

To Increase Difficulty

- Reduce the size of the target.
- Place fielders to guard the target.
- Get a more-challenging bowler to bowl at you.

To Decrease Difficulty

- Widen the target areas.
- Face a less-challenging bowler.

Success Check

- Ensure you have a good set-up with a high backlift.

- Move backwards to get into line while maintaining a side-on position and leaving your head behind.
- Have your top hand in control as you bring the bat down to strike the ball close to your body.
- At the completion of the stroke, make sure the blade of the bat points in the direction the ball has been hit, with the bat as an extension of your forearm.

Score Your Success

5 or 6 balls driven along the ground between the target cones = 5 points

3 or 4 balls driven along the ground between the target cones = 3 points

1 or 2 balls driven along the ground between the target cones = 1 point

Your Score ___

SWEEP

The sweep (figure 6.6, *a* and *b*) is a cross-batted shot played to a ball that is not full enough to drive but which can still be reached by a batsman moving forwards just after it pitches. A sweep usually is played to a ball pitching outside the leg stump. Proficient sweepers often ignore the line and sweep on length alone. However, if the ball is straight, you must be absolutely sure that you make some sort of contact with the bat, or you will be a prime candidate for an LBW dismissal. If the ball has pitched outside the leg stump, you cannot be out LBW; however, there is the possibility it will bounce unpredictably out of the rough created by a right-arm, over-the-wicket bowler at that end. The sweep is not without its perils, but it can be extremely effective in knocking a bowler off his rhythm.

With a sweep, your backlift needs to be high to counter any extra bounce. You want to hit the ball into the ground unless you are particularly proficient, there are no fielders in the deep on the leg side or the match situation demands that you take risks by taking the aerial route. Lead with your head towards the line of the ball; keep your front pad directly in line so that if you miss the ball, it will strike your pad. Bend your front leg at the knee; keep your back leg bent so that knee rests on the ground or just above it. Keep your weight forwards, with your head over the front knee to ensure that you are in a position to hit down on the ball. Aim just in front of square and bring the bat down in an arc, making contact at a full arm's stretch just after the ball pitches. At the completion of the stroke, your right shoulder should be pointing at the bowler.

Figure 6.6 Sweep

EXECUTION, FRONT VIEW
1. Use high backlift
2. Make contact with arms fully extended in front of front pad
3. Natural follow-through

a

EXECUTION, SIDE VIEW
1. Lead with head and front shoulder towards pitch of ball
2. Bend front knee
3. Keep head straight
4. Sweeping motion of bat

b

Misstep
You keep hitting sweeps in the air.

Correction
Make sure you hit down on the ball from a high backlift. Fully extend your arms when playing the shot.

It is important that you lead towards the ball with your head and front pad because there is little hope of making contact if you are inside the line of the ball. In that case, the ball would pass you, and your bat would have to catch up with it to make contact. That is why you should try to sweep in front of square, sometimes sending the ball backwards of square if you hit it later than intended.

Misstep
You do not make any contact when you go to sweep.

Correction
You are probably trying to play the ball too fine. Try to hit the ball just in front of square.

The sweep is usually played against slower bowlers because it takes perfect timing and no little courage to use it against anyone bowling at medium pace or above. Keep your head still throughout the execution of the shot; your head should be low down and directly in line with the ball. You need confidence in your ability to play a sweep; a half-hearted approach is unlikely to succeed with any consistency. Do not try to hit the ball too hard. That will topple you off balance. Without balance, your chances of success are severely impaired.

On occasion, you may deliberately try to sweep the ball in the air. Unattractively named a slog-sweep (figure 6.7), this stroke can be used by a batsman to exploit any gaps in the field. It should be played only when you are well set or the situation demands it, but it can prove a beneficial way of imposing authority over the bowler. Even though it is a very aggressive stroke, it is important to avoid trying to hit the ball too hard. Maintain your shape as you go down on one knee and try to hit up to dispatch the ball over mid-wicket. During the follow-through, the bat is in different plane than for a sweep along the ground, transcribing an arc that hits the ball in the air. This is a pleasing stroke to play, but it is a pity that there is not a more aesthetically pleasing way of describing it.

Figure 6.7   Slog-Sweep in the Air

EXECUTION

1. Go down on one knee
2. Maintain shape
3. Get under ball
4. Hit up

Sweep Drill 1.   *Imaginary Sweeps*

Play sweeps against an imaginary ball with either a coach or experienced partner watching or in front of a mirror. Shape to play six balls.

Success Check

- Ensure you have a good set-up with a high backlift.
- Lead with your head towards the pitch of the ball.
- Bend your front leg as you bring the bat down and across your body.

- Extend your arms as you try to play the ball just in front of square.

Score Your Success

5 or 6 well-executed drives = 5 points

3 or 4 well-executed drives = 3 points

1 or 2 well-executed drives = 1 point

Your Score ＿＿＿

Sweep Drill 2. *Target Sweeps*

Mark a target with two cones. Exactly where the target is depends on the room available. In an average-size sports hall, for example, the target can be on the back wall. A feeder delivers a ball. Attempt to sweep it between the cones and along the ground. Hit six balls.

To Increase Difficulty

- Reduce the size of the target.
- Place fielders to guard the target.

To Decrease Difficulty

- If you have difficulty hitting a moving ball, set the ball up on a high tee and drive it off the tee.
- Have the feeder drop the ball; sweep it after it bounces.

Success Check

- Ensure you have a good set-up with a high backlift.

- Lead with your head towards the pitch of the ball.
- Bend your front leg as you bring the bat down and across your body.
- Extend your arms as you try to play the ball just in front of square.

Score Your Success

5 or 6 balls swept along the ground between the target cones = 5 points

3 or 4 balls swept along the ground between the target cones = 3 points

1 or 2 balls swept along the ground between the target cones = 1 point

Your Score ___

Sweep Drill 3. *Full Delivery*

Put on full protection and have a bowler deliver six balls for you to sweep between target cones.

To Increase Difficulty

- Reduce the size of the target.
- Place fielders to guard the target.
- Get a more-challenging bowler to bowl at you.

To Decrease Difficulty

- Widen the target areas.
- Face a less-challenging bowler.

Success Check

- Ensure you have a good set-up with a high backlift.

- Lead with your head towards the pitch of the ball.
- Bend your front leg as you bring the bat down and across your body.
- Extend your arms as you try to play the ball just in front of square.

Score Your Success

5 or 6 balls driven along the ground between the target cones = 5 points

3 or 4 balls driven along the ground between the target cones = 3 points

1 or 2 balls driven along the ground between the target cones = 1 point

Your Score ___

SQUARE CUT

If you are faced with a ball that is short and wide of the off-stump and you have lifted your bat high, four runs are there for the taking with the square cut (figure 6.8, *a* and *b*). As its name implies, you want to play the ball square. If you are a little early in making contact, the ball will go in front of square; if you are slightly late, you should reach the boundary backwards of square. Because this is another cross-batted shot, it is sometimes regarded as risky; however, if it is well executed, it should not present too many problems.

For once, you do not need to get your head behind the line of the ball because the ball is too wide for that. You still should move your back foot and ensure that your weight—your head—is over that foot. The wider the ball, the more you want to move your back foot farther towards the off side. If the ball is closer to your body, move your foot farther back than across. Be careful about trying to play this shot if the ball is not sufficiently wide of off-stump. Otherwise, you may be cramped for room, risking a bottom edge onto the stumps or a top edge to give a catch behind the wicket. Any follow-through associated with this shot will be purely a natural finish. You do not want to check the follow-through, but neither should you attempt to hit the ball so hard that there is a great flourish of a follow-through. If that happens, you will not be able to control the stroke and will end up off balance.

Misstep
You give a catch to the wicket-keeper when playing the stroke.

Correction
This usually occurs when you try to cut a ball that is too close to you.

Figure 6.8   **Square Cut**

EXECUTION, FRONT VIEW

1. Use high backlift
2. Turn shoulder
3. Bring bat down to make contact with ball

a

(continued)

Figure 6.8 (continued)

EXECUTION, SIDE VIEW

1. Move back foot backwards and across, based on line of ball
2. Shift weight to back foot
3. Keep weight on back foot
4. Do not use deliberate follow-through
5. Allow bat to move through natural momentum

b

Misstep
When you play the cut shot, the ball goes in the air.

Correction
Make sure you play the shot from a high backlift, thereby playing down onto the ball.

As you move backwards, keep watching the ball but turn your front shoulder away so that its back is almost facing the bowler. This pushes your bat even higher, allowing you to bring it down with a full swing into the hitting zone. You can use the pace of the ball on the bat, so you do not need to hit it too hard. In fact you will lessen the chances of making good contact if you overexert yourself when playing the stroke. The bowler has done the hard work by putting pace on the ball and delivering it short and wide of the wicket. It is a bad ball that deserves to be punished; you, as the batsman, can take full advantage with minimal effort.

Misstep
You fail to make contact at all.

Correction
The most common cause is pushing a straight bat across the line of the ball. Make sure you play with a cross bat. Do not try to hit it too hard; instead, use the pace of the ball to get your power.

In addition to the square cut, you can run the ball finer towards third man by playing the late cut (figure 6.9, *a* and *b*). Instead of throwing the bat at the ball to hit it square on the off side, delay the stroke, especially against a slower bowler, to finesse it backwards of point. Move your back foot right back and watch the ball closely, so that you can run the ball off an angled bat in the direction you want it to go. You need not put any force into the stroke. Use the pace on the ball and timing to guide rather than hit it.

a

b

Figure 6.9 The late cut is very similar to the square cut, but the batsman brings the bat down on the ball later in its path to finesse it towards third man. (*a*) Front view; (*b*) side view.

Square Cut Drill 1. *Imaginary Square Cuts*

Play square cuts against an imaginary ball with either a coach or experienced partner watching or in front of a mirror. Shape to play six balls.

Success Check

- Ensure you have a good set-up with a high backlift.
- Move your back foot backwards and across towards the line of the ball, turning your front shoulder as you do to take the backlift higher.
- Bring the bat down on the ball with your arms extended.
- At the completion of the shot, make sure your weight is on your back foot.

Score Your Success

5 or 6 well-executed square cuts = 5 points

3 or 4 well-executed square cuts = 3 points

1 or 2 well-executed square cuts = 1 point

Your Score ___

Square Cut Drill 2. *Target Square Cuts*

Mark a target with two cones. Exactly where the target is depends on the room available. In an average-size sports hall, for example, the target can be on the back wall. The feeder delivers the ball. Attempt to cut it between the cones and along the ground. Hit six balls.

To Increase Difficulty

• Reduce the size of the target.

• Place fielders to guard the target.

To Decrease Difficulty

• Begin with the bat raised in the backlift and your weight already on your back foot, ensuring the feeder delivers the ball to the right place for you to hit.

Success Check

• Ensure you have a good set-up with a high backlift.

• Move your back foot backwards and across towards the line of the ball, turning your front shoulder as you do to take the backlift higher.

• Bring the bat down on the ball with your arms extended.

• At the completion of the shot, make sure your weight is on your back foot.

Score Your Success

5 or 6 balls cut along the ground between the target cones = 5 points

3 or 4 balls cut along the ground between the target cones = 3 points

1 or 2 balls cut along the ground between the target cones = 1 point

Your Score ___

Square Cut Drill 3. *Full Square Cuts*

Put on full protection and have a bowler deliver six balls for you to cut between target cones and along the ground.

To Increase Difficulty

• Reduce the size of the target.

• Place fielders to guard the target.

• Get a more-challenging bowler to bowl at you.

To Decrease Difficulty

• Widen the target areas.

• Face a less-challenging bowler.

Success Check

• Ensure you have a good set-up with a high backlift.

• Move your back foot backwards and across towards the line of the ball, turning your front shoulder as you do to take the backlift higher.

• Bring the bat down on the ball with your arms extended.

• At the completion of the shot, make sure your weight is on your back foot.

Score Your Success

5 or 6 balls cut along the ground between the target cones = 5 points

3 or 4 balls cut along the ground between the target cones = 3 points

1 or 2 balls cut along the ground between the target cones = 1 point

Your Score ___

PULL

There is an argument that the pull shot (figure 6.10, *a* and *b*) should be the easiest to play because it is perhaps the most natural. Throw a ball to a young child holding a bat, and he will swing the bat from off to leg to hit the ball in that direction. He may not know it at the time, but he is playing the pull shot. An older player needs to retain the uninhibited swing but apply a few basic requirements to keep his swing under control. And he needs to do is pick the right ball, one that is short a length down the leg side or even on the wicket.

The first movement is with your back foot, which moves backwards and, depending on how wide the ball is, possibly slightly outside the leg stump. Slightly is the key word: do not get outside the line of the ball. Your head should be right in line. Your front foot moves backwards to the same depth in the crease as your back foot. You are now chest-on to the bowler, with your head in front of your body so that you are hitting down on the ball. It is important to keep watching the ball so that you can adjust to any unpredictable bounce.

Misstep
If the bounce of the ball varies, you miss it completely.

Correction
You might be turning your head too early. Keep watching the point at which you make contact with the ball, and then you will not miss it.

Figure 6.10   Pull

EXECUTION, FRONT VIEW

1. Use high backlift
2. Move into chest-on position
3. Bring bat down to make contact at full stretch

a

(continued)

Figure 6.10 *(continued)*

EXECUTION, SIDE VIEW

1. Move back foot backwards
2. Throw front leg to leg side
3. Keep head behind line
4. Contact ball at full stretch in front of body
5. Follow-through along natural arc

b

 Misstep
The ball invariably goes past your body on the leg side without making contact with your bat.

Correction
You are not getting into the correct position to play the ball, or you are trying to hit it too fine. If you miss the ball, it should hit you. Try to hit it in front of square.

From a high backlift, bring the bat across your body and try to hit the ball at a full arm's stretch into an area between square leg and midwicket. At the completion of the shot, transfer your weight to your front leg; keep your head straight and still. Keep looking at the spot where your bat made contact with the ball. This may not be a natural thing to do, but it does prevent you from turning your head too early and taking your eye off the ball. As with most attacking strokes, the main problem when pulling is trying to hit the ball too hard. This will result in a loss of balance and shape.

 Misstep
You usually hit the ball in the air.

Correction
You have not used a high backlift and are hitting up instead of down onto the ball.

 Misstep
You have no control over the shot.

Correction
Do not try to hit the ball too hard.

Pull Drill 1. *Imaginary Pull Shots*

Play pull shots against an imaginary ball with either a coach or experienced partner watching or in front of a mirror. Shape to play six balls.

Success Check

- Ensure you have a good set-up with a high backlift.
- Move your front foot backwards and across to get your body in line with the imaginary ball.
- Bring the bat down with your arms extended.

- Keep watching the point at which you plan to make contact, rather than turning your head too early.
- At the completion of the shot, make sure your weight is on your front foot. Do not move your head to the leg side.

Score Your Success

5 or 6 well-executed pulls = 5 points

3 or 4 well-executed pulls = 3 points

1 or 2 well-executed pulls = 1 point

Your Score ___

Pull Drill 2. *Target Pull Shots*

Mark a target with two cones as shown in figure 6.11. The server bounces the ball in the designated area, in line with or just outside the line of the leg stump. The batsman plays a pull shot, aiming at the target area. The batsman attempts to pull the ball between the cones and along the ground. Hit six balls.

This layout can be adapted to practice all attacking strokes. Adjust the targets to fit whichever stroke is being practiced.

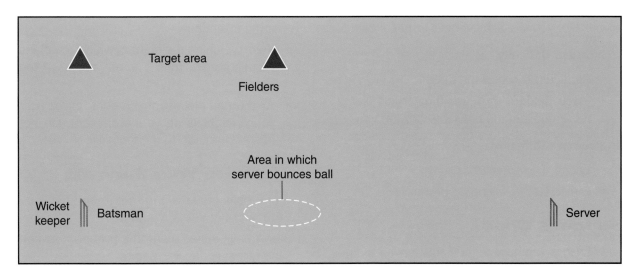

Figure 6.11   Set-up for target pull shots.

(continued)

Pull Drill 2. *(continued)*

To Increase Difficulty

- Reduce the size of the target.
- Place fielders to guard the target area. Make sure fielders are far enough away from the batsman to be out of danger.
- The batsman runs to the stumps on the server's end and back before the fielders return the ball to the wicket-keeper.

To Decrease Difficulty

- Begin with the bat raised in the backlift and your body already in position, ensuring the feeder delivers the ball in the right place for you to hit.

Success Check

- Ensure you have a good set-up with a high backlift.

- Move your front foot backwards and across to get your body in line with the ball.
- Bring the bat down on the ball with your arms extended.
- Keep watching the point at which you make contact, rather than turning your head too early.
- At the completion of the shot, make sure your weight is on your front foot. Do not move your head to the leg side.

Score Your Success

5 or 6 balls pulled along the ground between the target cones = 5 points

3 or 4 balls pulled along the ground between the target cones = 3 points

1 or 2 balls pulled along the ground between the target cones = 1 point

Your Score ___

Pull Drill 3. *Game-Like Pull Shots*

Put on full protection and have a bowler deliver six balls for you to pull between a target of cones.

To Increase Difficulty

- Reduce the size of the target.
- Place fielders to guard the target* Get a more-challenging bowler to bowl at you.

To Decrease Difficulty

- Widen the target areas.
- Face a less-challenging bowler.

Success Check

- Ensure you have a good set-up with a high backlift.
- Move your front foot backwards and across to get your body in line with the ball.

- Bring the bat down on the ball with your arms extended.
- Keep watching the point at which you make contact, rather than turning your head too early.
- At the completion of the shot, make sure your weight is on your front foot. Do not move your head to the leg side.

Score Your Success

5 or 6 balls pulled along the ground between the target cones = 5 points

3 or 4 balls pulled along the ground between the target cones = 3 points

1 or 2 balls pulled along the ground between the target cones = 1 point

Your Score ___

HOOK

In contrast to the pull, which is played to a short, leg-side ball that rises to about chest height from a medium pace bowler or spinner, the hook (figure 6.12) is a response to a short ball from a quicker bowler that has bounced up between chest and head height on the leg side. Attempt a hook only when well set because it can be risky if you try it before you have had time to adjust to the conditions and the bowler. You also need to know where the fielders are because, given variable bounce, it is not always possible to play this shot down. You are better advised to duck or sway out of the way unless you are confident that you can avoid any fielders positioned to catch an unwary hooker.

Misstep

You always hook the ball straight up in the air without any control.

Correction

You are probably trying to hook a ball that is too far to the off. Let it go.

Once you decide to hook, as soon as you see that short ball bouncing towards your head, move backwards and pivot on your back leg, bringing your head inside the line at the critical moment so that if you miss the ball it will pass harmlessly over your front shoulder. From your high backlift, bring the bat across your body in front of your eyes and help the ball towards the boundary between square leg and fine leg.

Misstep

You get hit every time you go to hook.

Correction

Make sure you get inside the line so that the ball passes over your front shoulder if you miss it.

Figure 6.12   Hook

EXECUTION

1. Move back to get your head just inside line of ball
2. Pivot on back leg
3. Make contact as ball passes over front shoulder
4. Pivot completely around
5. Hit ball behind square on leg side

You sometimes hear of rolling your wrists when you hook, but there is usually insufficient time to complete this manoeuvre. You can try to hook down if the ball has not climbed too high, or you can deliberately attempt to hit it in the air for six. Balance is the key to controlling this stroke. It carries a high degree of risk, but it is also a means of taking the game to the bowler. It is up to you to assess the percentages and decide if they are in your favour at any particular stage of the game.

Misstep
Whenever you try to hook, you get caught at long leg.

Correction
Give up playing the stroke if the percentages of success are not in your favour.

Hook Drill 1. *Imaginary Hook Shots*

Play hook shots against an imaginary ball with either a coach or experienced partner watching or in front of a mirror. Shape to hook six balls.

Success Check

- Ensure you have a good set-up with a high backlift.
- Move your back foot backwards to get your body inside the line of the imaginary ball.
- Pivot round as you play the shot as if you are helping the ball on its way.

- For two imaginary balls, instead of going through the shape of the hook, get out of the way, either ducking down or swaying back.

Score Your Success

5 or 6 well-executed hooks or leaves = 5 points

3 or 4 well-executed hooks or leaves = 3 points

1 or 2 well-executed hooks or leaves = 1 point

Your Score ____

Hook Drill 2. *Hooking Tennis Balls*

Have a feeder deliver tennis balls towards your head. Attempt to hook, duck underneath or sway out of their way. Take six balls.

To Increase Difficulty

- Increase the speed of the service. In order to increase the speed considerably, the feeder can use a tennis racket to feed the ball.
- Put fielders in position to take the catch.

To Decrease Difficulty

- Decrease the speed of the service to give you more time to make a decision and execute the shot.

Success Check

- Ensure you have a good set-up with a high backlift.

- Move your back foot backwards to get your body inside the line of the ball.
- Pivot around as you make contact with the ball so you are helping it on its way.
- If you decide not to hook, duck underneath the ball, getting your hands and bat out of the way, or sway inside or outside the line.

Score Your Success

5 or 6 balls hooked or successfully avoided = 5 points

3 or 4 balls hooked or successfully avoided = 3 points

1 or 2 balls hooked or successfully avoided = 1 point

Your Score ___

Hook Drill 3. *Full Hook Shots*

Put on full protection and have a bowler deliver six balls for you to hook. You can go through with the shot, or you can sway or duck out of the way. Play six balls.

To Increase Difficulty

- Position fielders to take possible catches.
- Increase the pace of the delivery.

To Decrease Difficulty

- Have the bowler bowl very short but not too quickly, giving you time to play or leave.

Success Check

- Ensure you have a good set-up with a high backlift.

- Move your back foot backwards to get your body inside the line of the ball.
- Pivot around as you make contact with the ball so you are helping it on its way.
- If you decide not to hook, duck underneath the ball, getting your hands and bat out of the way, or sway inside or outside the line.

Score Your Success

5 or 6 balls successfully hooked or left = 5 points

3 or 4 balls successfully hooked or left = 3 points

1 or 2 balls successfully hooked or left = 1 point

Your Score ___

LEG GLANCE

You can work the ball away on the leg side for the easy run that keeps the board ticking over without much risk. You can do this off the back or front foot. The leg glance (figure 6.13, *a* and *b*) is particularly useful early in your innings against quicker bowlers because you can use the pace they provide.

If the ball is of a good length, pitching around leg stump, lead with your head towards the line.

If the ball has pitched outside leg stump, put your front pad between it and the stumps. As you lean into the ball and your straight bat makes contact with it, angle your bat down towards square leg by using your wrists and nudge the ball into a gap in the field. Be careful not to close the bat face too early; otherwise, the ball may hit the leading edge and present an easy catch.

Misstep

You frequently give a catch from a leading edge when playing the leg glance.

Correction

You are turning the bat too early. Wait for the ball to come up. Make contact before turning your wrists.

Figure 6.13   Leg Glance off Front Foot

EXECUTION, FRONT VIEW

1. Bring straight bat down onto ball
2. Turn wrists at contact
3. Glance ball away on leg side

a

EXECUTION, SIDE VIEW

1. Lead with head and front shoulder towards line of ball or just inside it
2. Keep front foot in natural position

b

Playing the ball off your back foot is similar. Allow a ball pitching short of a length on the leg side, but not bouncing very much, to come up to your hip before you turn it away. This is a relatively simple way to add runs. Move backwards, using the depth of the crease, with your head forward and over the line of the ball; bring your hands down towards the ball with your bat angled down (figure 6.14, *a* and *b*). You then simply turn the bat face to help the ball on its way.

Figure 6.14 Leg Glance off Back Foot

MOVE BACKWARDS

1. Move backwards to get in line of ball or just inside it

a

(continued)

Figure 6.14 *(continued)*

ANGLE BAT

1. Allow ball to come to you
2. Angle bat by turning wrists
3. Send ball away to leg side

b

Misstep
You fail to make contact with the ball when you attempt the leg glance off either the back foot or the front foot.

Correction
You are moving too far inside the line of the ball rather than moving into the line.

Misstep
You hit the ball up in the air rather than playing it down.

Correction
Make sure you have a high backlift. When you are glancing off the front foot, lead out with your head over the ball as you make contact. When you are glancing off the back foot, let the ball come up and play it from under your head.

Leg Glance Drill 1. *Imaginary Leg Glances*

Play leg glances against an imaginary ball with either a coach or experienced partner watching or in front of a mirror. Shape to glance six balls, three off the back foot and three off the front foot.

Success Check

- Ensure you have a good set-up with a high backlift.
- To glance off the front foot, lead with your head towards the line of the imaginary ball.

- To glance off the back foot, move backwards into line, with your head over the imaginary ball.
- At the moment of contact, turn your wrists.

Score Your Success

5 or 6 well-executed glances = 5 points

3 or 4 well-executed glances = 3 points

1 or 2 well-executed glances = 1 point

Your Score ___

Leg Glance Drill 2. *Tennis Ball Leg Glances*

Have a feeder deliver a tennis ball that is either down the leg side and of a good length or just short of a length. Attempt to play the ball between the cones using a leg glance. Play six balls.

To Increase Difficulty

- Mix up the length of ball so you have to decide whether to go forwards or backwards to play the stroke.
- Set up a number of targets to which the ball must be played.

To Decrease Difficulty

- Have the feeder tell you in advance whether you will be receiving a ball to glance off the back or front foot.

Success Check

- Ensure you have a good set-up with a high backlift.

- To glance off your front foot, lead with your head towards the line of the ball.
- To glance off your back foot, move backwards into line with your head over the ball.
- Allow the ball to come to you rather than push at it with firm hands.
- At the moment of contact, turn your wrists to direct the ball into a gap in the field.

Score Your Success

5 or 6 balls glanced along the ground into the target area = 5 points

3 or 4 balls glanced along the ground into the target area = 3 points

1 or 2 balls glanced along the ground into the target area = 1 point

Your Score ___

Leg Glance Drill 3. *Full Leg Glances*

Put on full protection and have a bowler deliver six balls for you to glance. You can play off the front or back foot, depending on the length of the ball.

To Increase Difficulty

- Position fielders to take possible catches.
- Increase the pace of the delivery.

To Decrease Difficulty

- Have a less-challenging bowler tell you in advance whether you will need to move forwards or backwards.

Success Check

- Ensure you have a good set-up with a high backlift.

- To glance off the front foot, lead with your head towards the line of the ball.
- To glance off the back foot, move backwards into line with your head over the ball.
- Allow the ball to come to you rather than push at it with firm hands.
- At the moment of contact, turn your wrists to direct the ball into a gap in the field.

Score Your Success

5 or 6 balls successfully glanced = 5 points

3 or 4 balls successfully glanced = 3 points

1 or 2 balls successfully glanced = 1 point

Your Score ___

BATTING STRATEGIES

Steps 4, 5, and 6 cover basic batting, defensive batting and attacking batting. After developing the skills described in these three steps, you will have the strokes to deal with all balls that are bowled at you. Awareness of the match situation should determine your approach. You react to the ball that is bowled. With practice and sufficient thought, you should be able to automatically respond to any ball bowled. Once you get to that point, all you need to do is execute the appropriate shot, which should itself be honed to perfection by meaningful practice.

To get used to the idea of reacting to the ball, rather than predetermining the stroke and hoping that the bowler delivers the ball in the right place, consider table 6.1.

As alternatives, you can play the leg glance off the front or back foot, or you can play a late cut.

In addition, there is always the leave. You always have that option once you have determined which strokes fit easily into your repertoire and which are likely to reduce the probability of your success.

To summarise, if your set-up—grip, stance and backlift—is good, you can concentrate on the ball and watch it all the way from the bowler's hand. If you judge the line and length so that you can select the correct shot, all you have to do is execute that shot well. Being able to do that will come with diligent practice. After all these skills and decisions are second nature, all that remains is to practice how to acknowledge your hundred!

Table 6.1 Batting Strategy Based on Ball Bowled

Ball bowled	Best batting option	Step and page number
Good length ball threatening the stumps	Forward defensive	Step 5, page 62
Ball just short of a length threatening the stumps	Backward defensive	Step 5, page 67
Overpitched straight ball	Straight drive	Step 6, page 81
Overpitched ball on the leg side	On-drive	Step 6, page 76
Overpitched ball on the off side	Off-drive	Step 6, page 76
Overpitched ball a little wider on the off side	Cover drive	Step 6, page 76
Straight ball just short of a length and not bouncing	Straight drive off the back foot	Step 6, page 83
Ball just short of a length on the leg side and not bouncing	On-drive off the back foot	Step 6, page 83
Ball just short of a length on the off side and not bouncing	Off-drive off the back foot	Step 6, page 83
Short ball on the leg side off spinner or medium pacer	Pull	Step 6, page 95
Short ball on the leg side off quicker bowler	Hook	Step 6, page 99
Short ball on the off side	Square cut	Step 6, page 91

Batting Drill 1. *Imaginary Batting*

Shape to play all the attacking strokes again an imaginary ball with either a coach or experienced partner watching or in front of a mirror. Shape to play 12 balls, going through all the strokes mentioned in this step. If you have a partner, he can decide which stroke you must demonstrate.

Success Check

• Ensure you have a good set-up with a high backlift.

• Refer to the individual strokes so that you know the shape you are aiming for.

Score Your Success

11 or 12 well-executed strokes = 10 points

8 to 10 well-executed strokes = 7 points

1 to 7 well-executed strokes = 3 points

Your Score ___

Batting Drill 2. *Hitting a Tennis Ball*

Have a feeder deliver a tennis ball against which you play the appropriate attacking stroke determined by line and length. Play 12 balls.

To Increase Difficulty

• Increase the pace of the delivery.

• Set up a number of targets to which the ball must be played.

To Decrease Difficulty

• Have the feeder tell you in advance what sort of delivery he is going to make so that you can preset yourself for the appropriate stroke.

Success Check

• Ensure you have a good set-up with a high backlift.

• Refer to the individual strokes so that you know the shape you are aiming for.

Score Your Success

11 or 12 well-executed strokes = 10 points

8 to 10 well-executed strokes = 7 points

1 to 7 well-executed strokes = 3 points

Your Score ____

Batting Drill 3. *Full Batting*

Put on full protection and have a bowler deliver 12 balls for you to play. Depending on the length and line of the ball, decide on the appropriate stroke.

To Increase Difficulty

• Position fielders to take possible catches.

• Increase the pace of the delivery.

To Decrease Difficulty

• Have a less-challenging bowler tell you in advance what sort of ball he is going to bowl.

Success Check

• Ensure you have a good set-up with a high backlift.

• Refer to the individual strokes so that you know the shape you are aiming for.

Score Your Success

11 or 12 well-executed strokes = 10 points

8 to 10 well-executed strokes = 7 points

1 to 7 well-executed strokes = 3 points

Your Score ____

SUCCESS SUMMARY OF ATTACKING BATTING

The key to attacking batting is shot selection. Provided you have mastered the basics of batting and have good defensive techniques to deal with those balls that should not be attacked (except in situations when all balls must be attacked), the next problem is determining which stroke to play. Try to compartmentalise your mind so that as soon as you see a half volley, you drive it; when you see a short ball outside off-stump, you cut it; and so on. Refer to the chart on page 107. But remember, if the ball is short, go backwards; if the ball is well pitched up, go forwards. Do not try to play every stroke described in this step. For example, if you are hitting on-drives in the air, cut that stroke out of your repertoire until you have done more work to perfect it. Think about glancing instead. If you are not good at hooking, make sure you can get out of the way of a short ball aimed at your upper body.

Before moving on to step 7, Fielding, evaluate how you did on the attacking batting drills in this step. Tally your scores to determine how well you have mastered the skill of attacking batting. If you scored 100 points, you are ready to move on to step 7. If you did not score 100 points, practice the drills again until you raise your scores before moving on to step 7.

Front-Foot Drive Drills

1. Imaginary Front-Foot Drives   ___ out of 5

2. Target Front-Foot Drives   ___ out of 5

3. Mix It Up   ___ out of 5

Back-Foot Drive Drills

1. Imaginary Back-Foot Drives   ___ out of 5

2. Target Back-Foot Drives   ___ out of 5

3. Mix It Up   ___ out of 5

Sweep Drills

1. Imaginary Sweeps   ___ out of 5

2. Target Sweeps   ___ out of 5

3. Full Delivery   ___ out of 5

Square Cut Drills

1. Imaginary Square Cuts   ___ out of 5

2. Target Square Cuts   ___ out of 5

3. Full Square Cuts   ___ out of 5

(continued)

(continued)

Pull Drills

1. Imaginary Pull Shots   ___ out of 5

2. Target Pull Shots   ___ out of 5

3. Game-Like Pull Shots   ___ out of 5

Hook Drills

1. Imaginary Hook Shots   ___ out of 5

2. Hooking Tennis Balls   ___ out of 5

3. Full Hook Shots   ___ out of 5

Leg Glance Drills

1. Imaginary Leg Glances   ___ out of 5

2. Tennis Ball Leg Glances   ___ out of 5

3. Full Leg Glances   ___ out of 5

Batting Drills

1. Imaginary Batting   ___ out of 10

2. Hitting a Tennis Ball   ___ out of 10

3. Full Batting   ___ out of 10

Total   ___ **out of 135**

Whether you are a specialist batsman or bowler, you will spend a lot of time fielding. It is important to become a good fielder so you can play your full part on the team. A good fielding side is usually a successful side, so you need to ensure that you are as proficient as possible in this area of cricket. Take all the advice you are about to get in step 7, and you will be well on your way to achieving that goal.

Fielding

Catches win matches is one of the oldest clichés in cricket, but time has not diminished its truth. A side no better than ordinary in other aspects of cricket can be transformed into a useful team by achieving a higher standard of fielding. Catches do win matches, just as dropped catches can lose them, and ground fielding is also important in determining the outcome.

Despite these proven tenets, for many years fielding was disregarded when it came to developing cricketers. Natural athletes were seen to add value to the team in the field, but the true value of improving fielding skills was not appreciated. Attention was focused on batting and bowling. It was the advent of one-day cricket at the highest level that underlined the need for good fielders. It slowly dawned on players and coaches that a proficient batsman or bowler who was a liability in the field could not command a place in the team. All players have since had to reach an acceptable standard of all-round fielding ability; more work has been done to ensure that each member of the team, even if not a natural gazelle, reaches an acceptable standard of mobility, catching and throwing.

Across all levels of cricket, it is now the good fielder who gets the nod when other factors cannot separate players vying for the same place in a side. Players work on their fielding skills, and coaches develop new methods to help them improve. The climate of indifference towards fielding has dissipated so that anyone who fails to reach a minimum standard in the field is embarrassed for himself and looked down upon by team-mates.

Various elements of fielding require study to succeed at this vital step in cricketing success. You need to be able to move properly to stop the ball or chase after it. You need to be able to throw. You need to be able to catch the ball. You will spend more of a match fielding than you will batting or bowling, so it is important to use this time profitably. If you hide and hope the ball never comes your way, you are unlikely to enjoy the game as a whole. If you want the ball to come to you so that you can demonstrate your fielding skills, you will get so much more from cricket.

INTERCEPTING

The first job of a fielder is to keep the ball from getting past him. If the ball is in the air, you want to catch it; if it is along the ground, you still have an important job to do. There used to be a differentiation between attacking and defensive fielding, but as the game has progressed, all fielding should be undertaken with attack in mind. Even when fielding in the deep, get to the ball as quickly as possible and return it to the stumps with similar rapidity.

This rule applies to what might be thought of as the most defensive way of stopping the ball: the long barrier. To make absolutely sure that the ball will not get past you on even the bumpiest of outfields, go down on one knee and use the length of your leg as an extra line of defence

should the ball evade your hands. Hence the term *long barrier*. Before using this technique, save time by moving towards the ball so you intercept it before it travels towards your position, which is probably on the boundary.

As soon as you have judged the line of the ball, race in to meet it as close to the stumps as you can. When you meet the ball, form a long barrier by going down on one knee and using the length of your leg as an extra line of defence. A right-handed thrower goes down so that his left knee is on the ground; a left-handed thrower goes down on his right knee. You will be able to get up into a throwing position more easily if you use the correct leg to form your barrier. Every second is crucial.

Misstep

When using the long barrier, you take a long time to get into the throwing position.

Correction

You are going down on the wrong knee. Right-handed throwers should go down on their left knees so that they can stand straight up to throw. Left-handed throwers should go down on their right knees.

But there is more to it than going down on the correct knee. Make sure your head is right over the line of the ball; this will allow you to adjust more easily than if you are looking askance at the ball. Hold your hands with fingers pointing

down in line with the ball, which should come to rest in your grasp (figure 7.1*a*). When the ball is in your hands, and not before, rise to the throwing position, take aim and fire (figure 7.1*b*).

Figure 7.1   Long Barrier

KNEEL AND SECURE THE BALL

1. Go down on left knee (right-handed thrower)
2. Keep left knee next to right heel
3. Point fingers down
4. Receive ball with fingers down
5. Keep head over line of ball
6. Watch ball into hands

a

RISE AND THROW

1. Rise to side-on position
2. Hold throwing arm back and ready to throw
3. Hold non-throwing arm out, seeking target

b

Misstep
Despite using the long barrier, the ball still gets past you.

Correction
Consider whether you are really making a long barrier. Perhaps you have left a gap between your knee on the ground and your heel, or your leg is not on the ground or your leg is at the wrong angle so that it is not 90 degrees to the line of the ball.

The long barrier technique usually is used when you are fielding close to the boundary. Your first objective is to stop the ball from crossing the rope. If you are a little closer in, you want to put pressure on the batsmen by attempting to run them out. At this range, some 40 yards (36.6 m) or so from the stumps, you will be too far away to execute an underarm throw but are risking that the ball may bobble on the outfield and go past you. Still, you should apply good technique to give yourself the best possible chance of stopping the ball before concentrating on the run-out possibility.

When you are in the field, anticipate that the ball will come to you and be ready to move. Most fielders walk in as the bowler delivers, but some adopt the position taken by a goalkeeper facing a penalty: weight balanced and ready to pounce. If fielders are in the latter category, they usually will have walked in a few paces, ready to go one way or the other. Once you have determined where the ball is going, move as quickly as possible towards it, timing your step pattern to arrive with your head over the ball as it reaches the same side of your body as your throwing arm. Bend down and watch the ball into your hands. Use a one- or two-handed intercept (figure 7.2, *a* and *b*). Then, with a fluid movement, come up into the throwing position and send the ball on a straight trajectory towards the target. Stay low even after releasing the ball (figure 7.3, *a* and *b*).

a   b

Figure 7.2 *(a)* For a one-handed intercept, the fielder picks up the ball in his right hand alongside his right foot; *(b)* for a two-handed intercept, the fielder watches the ball into both hands.

a   b

Figure 7.3 *(a)* The fielder draws back his throwing hand while his head and momentum move towards the target. *(b)* He says low even after releasing the ball.

Misstep

When using the two-handed intercept, you find that you cannot get down to pick up the ball because your front leg gets in the way.

Correction

You are getting your front foot in line with the ball rather than approaching the ball so that you can pick it up to the throwing side of your body.

Closer in, say 20 yards (18.3 m) from the stumps, you will not need to lift the ball up for an overarm throw at the target. You are in range for a fast underarm throw at the stumps aimed at running out the batsman. Speed is of the essence, but no matter how quick over the ground you are, your speed must be allied to accuracy. Move to intercept the ball in the right manner. Get low early so that as you reach the point of interception, you are crouching over the ball as it comes into your throwing hand; your fingers, as ever, are pointing down.

Misstep

It takes too long to get the ball back to the wicket-keeper when you use a one-handed intercept because you need time to adjust after stopping the ball.

Correction

Make sure you approach the ball so that your fingers are pointing down, with the palm of your hand, not the back, facing the target.

Your head is also a major consideration. Your head should move in the direction you want the ball to go after you pick it up. Get low early and stay low to prevent your head, and therefore your body weight, from bobbing down to the ball and then up again. Instead, watch the ball into the hand that is alongside the outside of your foot. Take one step to give your body impetus as you bring your hand back; then launch the ball towards the target. If your head is moving in the right direction, the ball should, too. If you got low and stayed low, there should be little danger of throwing the ball too high.

Hitting the target with the batsman out of his ground can be a match-turning moment. Just to save time, some fielders who are at close range actually launch themselves as well as the ball towards the target. The object is to get the ball in as quickly as possible. You will probably have to hit the stumps because there is often little chance of the wicket-keeper or bowler getting there in time to take a return.

Misstep

Although you make a good intercept with one hand, the subsequent throw usually goes over the wicket-keeper's head.

Correction

Get low early on your approach to the ball and keep low until after you have released the ball.

Intercept Drill 1. *Long-Barrier Intercepts*

Stand some 50 yards (45.7 m) away from your target, a wicket-keeper who stands behind a set of stumps. Have a feeder send the ball towards you with enough force to reach you. Use the long barrier to stop the ball and throw it to the wicket-keeper. Attempt six intercepts.

To Increase Difficulty

- Run in more quickly to meet the ball earlier to decrease the length of the subsequent throw; make sure your technique remains good despite the increase in speed.

To Decrease Difficulty

- Have the feeder use a slower feed.
- Use the long barrier to pick up a stationary ball and throw a shorter distance.

Success Check

- Once you have judged the line, go to meet the ball.

- With your head over the line of the ball, go down on the correct knee.
- Collect the ball with your fingers pointing down.
- Get up to throw the ball accurately to the wicket-keeper.

Score Your Success

5 or 6 successful intercepts using the long barrier = 5 points

3 or 4 successful intercepts using the long barrier = 3 points

1 or 2 successful intercepts using the long barrier = 1 point

Your Score ___

Intercept Drill 2. *Two-Handed Intercepts*

Stand 30 yards (27.4 m) away from your target, a wicket-keeper who stands by a set of stumps. Have a feeder send the ball towards you. Use a two-handed intercept to stop the ball and throw it to the wicket-keeper. Attempt six two-handed intercepts.

To Increase Difficulty

- Have the feeder deliver the ball a little wider than usual to force you to cover more ground before intercepting.

To Decrease Difficulty

- Have the feeder use a slower feed.
- Use a two-handed intercept to pick up a stationary ball.

Success Check

- Once you have judged the line, go to meet the ball.

- With your head over the line of the ball, allow room to let the ball pass beside your body.
- Collect the ball with your fingers pointing down alongside your body.
- Draw back your throwing arm to despatch the ball accurately to the wicket-keeper.

Score Your Success

5 or 6 successful two-handed intercepts = 5 points

3 or 4 successful two-handed intercepts = 3 points

1 or 2 successful two-handed intercepts = 1 point

Your Score ___

Intercept Drill 3. *One-Handed Intercepts*

Stand 15 yards (13.7 m) away from your target, a wicket-keeper who stands by a set of stumps. Have a feeder send the ball towards you. Use a one-handed intercept to stop the ball and throw it to the wicket-keeper. Attempt six one-handed intercepts.

To Increase Difficulty

- Have the feeder deliver the ball to one side or the other to force you to cover more ground before intercepting.
- Try to hit the stumps rather than return the ball to the wicket-keeper.

To Decrease Difficulty

- Have the feeder deliver the ball slowly straight to you.
- Pick up and throw a stationary ball.

Success Check

- Once you have judged the line, go to meet the ball.

- Try to adjust your step to pick up the ball on the throwing side of your body alongside your foot.
- Get low early and stay low.
- Collect the ball with your fingers pointing down.
- Take one step as you draw back your throwing arm; throw the ball underarm either at the stumps or to the wicket-keeper.

Score Your Success

5 or 6 successful one-handed intercepts = 5 points

3 or 4 successful one-handed intercepts = 3 points

1 or 2 successful one-handed intercepts = 1 point

Your Score ___

Intercept Drill 4. *Mixed Intercepts*

A feeder stands at the bowler's stumps and a wicket-keeper stands at the other set of stumps. The feeder delivers six balls to you. Intercept each with a long barrier: three balls with a two-handed intercept and three with a one-handed intercept. As each ball is on its way to you, the feeder shouts randomly, 'Bowler's end' or 'Wicket-keeper'; you have to make the intercept and return the ball to the nominated end.

To Increase Difficulty

- The feeder makes the call more quickly so you have less time to react.
- The feeder stands farther away from you so you have to move to your right or left to intercept.

To Decrease Difficulty

- The feeder tells you in advance the end to which each throw should go.

- The feeder serves each ball straight to you.

Success Check

- Refer to the section on each type of intercept in order to refresh the key elements of technique involved.

Score Your Success

5 or 6 successful intercepts and returns = 5 points

3 or 4 successful intercepts and returns = 3 points

1 or 2 successful intercepts and returns = 1 point

Your Score ___

RETRIEVING

However good you are at intercepting the ball, there will be times when the ball will get past you, forcing you to give chase. Naturally, you will want to catch up with the ball before it reaches the boundary—and the sooner the better. But it is not enough to simply hare after it without some idea of what you are going to do when you have caught up with it. There is a technique for getting the ball back to the stumps as quickly and accurately as possible.

After having caught up with the ball, position yourself so you can reach down with your throwing hand to pick it up (figure 7.4a) or, if it is still moving, allow it to run into your fingers. If you are at the boundary edge, you might have to flick the ball back into the playing field to prevent yourself from carrying it over the line; other times, you might have to slide and flick it back into the playing field. If you have time to stop before the boundary, do so as quickly as possible and turn away from your throwing arm. For example, a right-handed thrower will turn his body to his left (figure 7.4b), putting him in the throwing position much more quickly than by turning to the right.

As you turn, start getting into the throwing position by drawing back the hand that now has the ball in it; at the same time, your other hand seeks the target (figure 7.4c). If you are particularly athletic, you can turn and throw in one fluid movement, sometimes lifting yourself off the ground as you do so. However, it is normally advisable to establish a balanced position before you throw in order to gain distance and accuracy. If you have dived for the ball, your balanced position might be on your knees. Follow-through after releasing the ball (figure 7.4d).

Misstep
After you have reached the ball and picked it up, you have to spin around before getting the throw away.

Correction
Make sure you turn in the correct direction—away from your throwing arm.

Figure 7.4　Retrieving

STILL BALL

1. Get to ball as quickly as possible
2. Reach down with throwing hand to pick up ball

a

TURN

1. Pick up ball
2. Turn away from throwing arm

b

THROW

1. Draw back throwing arm
2. Seek target with non-throwing arm

c

(continued)

Figure 7.4 *(continued)*

FOLLOW-THROUGH

1. Release ball
2. Bring throwing arm through towards target

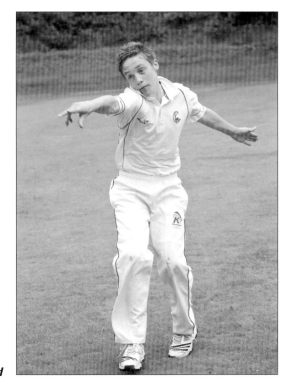

d

Misstep
It takes you too long to get the throw away after picking up the ball.

Correction
Do not overrun the ball. Pick up the ball, take a steadying step if necessary and immediately turn and throw.

Retrieving Drill 1. *Chase and Retrieve*

Stand alongside the wicket-keeper. The wicket-keeper rolls the ball out away from you for more than 25 yards (23.9 m). Chase after the ball, pick it up, turn and throw it back to the wicket-keeper. Retrieve six balls.

To Increase Difficulty

• The wicket-keeper feeds the ball faster so the chase and throw are longer.

To Decrease Difficulty

• The wicket-keeper feeds the ball more slowly, resulting in a shorter chase and throw.

Success Check

• Chase after the ball as quickly as possible.

• Reach down with your throwing arm, allowing the ball to roll into your hand with your fingers pointing down.

• Stop as quickly as possible and turn away from your throwing arm.

• Return the ball accurately to the wicket-keeper.

Score Your Success

5 or 6 retrieves = 5 points

3 or 4 retrieves = 3 points

1 or 2 retrieves = 1 point

Your Score ___

Retrieving Drill 2. *Chase and Return to Called End*

A feeder stands at the bowler's stumps, and a wicket-keeper stands at the other set of stumps. The feeder delivers six balls to you to chase and retrieve over varying distances up to 50 yards (45.7 m). As you chase each ball, the feeder shouts, 'Bowler's end' or 'Wicket-keeper'. Retrieve the ball and return it to the called end.

To Increase Difficulty

• The feeder makes the call later so you have less time to react.

• Increase the length of the chase.

To Decrease Difficulty

• The feeder tells you in advance the end to which each throw should go.

• Reduce the distance of the chase.

Success Check

• Chase after the ball as quickly as possible.

• Reach down with your throwing arm, allowing the ball to roll into your hand with your fingers pointing down.

• Stop as quickly as possible and turn away from your throwing arm.

• Return the ball accurately to the wicket-keeper.

Score Your Success

5 or 6 successful retrieves and returns = 5 points

3 or 4 successful retrieves and returns = 3 points

1 or 2 successful retrieves and returns = 1 point

Your Score ___

CATCHING

The three main types of catches are high catches, flat catches and catches taken close to the wicket. All require you to watch the ball closely as it goes into your hands and to close your hands securely round the ball once it is caught. Catching requires confidence. If you get tense and nervous, the chances of success diminish. Nobody drops a catch on purpose. As long as you make the best effort possible, nobody can criticise you. However, it takes a certain mental strength to come back from missing a catch to take the next one that comes your way. As with every other aspect of the game, sound technique gives you the best chance of success.

follow these steps, you should catch a lot more than you drop. The first step is to get into the right position, directly under where the ball is going to land (figure 7.5a). When you are fielding in the deep, and you see the ball hoisted in your direction, you may have a tendency to run in. If you do, the ball may go over your head, and you will have to backpedal frantically in an attempt to salvage the catch. When you see the ball go up, steady yourself for a moment in order to judge the trajectory before moving. It might even be a good idea to say the word *trajectory* to yourself to avoid rushing off in the wrong direction.

High Catches

Standing under a high catch is one of cricket's more daunting experiences. Nevertheless, if you

Misstep
High catches frequently go over your head.

Correction
Wait to judge the trajectory before moving. Do not run in as soon as you see the ball in the air unless you are certain that it is going to drop well short of you.

Figure 7.5 **Catching a High Ball**

WATCH BALL INTO HANDS

1. Judge trajectory of ball
2. Stand directly under where ball would land
3. Take balanced position
4. Hold hands outstretched and horizontal to ground
5. Point fingers away from you
6. Keep hands butted together
7. Watch ball into hands above eye level

a

CLOSE HAND OVER BALL

1. Catch ball in strongest hand
2. Close other hand over top once ball is safe
3. Bend elbows and pass them by sides
4. Clasp ball to chest

b

Once you have judged the flight of the ball, move towards it as quickly as possible. Try to achieve a balanced position so that you can watch the ball into your hands above eye level. This is important for two reasons. First you will be able to watch the ball right into your hands. If you catch it lower, you will not be able to watch the ball because it will speed past your line of sight as it drops into your hands. Second, if you attempt to catch the ball above the level of your eyes and it pops out of your grasp, you have a chance to make another attempt before it reaches the ground.

Misstep
You get into position to take a high catch, but you fail to hold the ball.

Correction
Make sure you are catching the ball above eye level. This means that you will be able to watch the ball right into your hands.

The conventional way of taking a high catch is with your hands outstretched and horizontal to the ground, palms up, and your fingers pointing away from you. Make sure that your hands are butted together; otherwise you leave a gap for the ball to go through. Because the join between your hands is the weakest point of the cup receiving the ball, ideally you will catch it in your strongest hand and close the other one over the top once the ball is safely held (figure 7.5b). When you have made the catch, allow your elbows to bend to pass either side of your body and clasp the ball to your chest. This giving motion will prevent you from presenting stiff hands to the ball, which might cause the ball to bounce out.

The other way to take a high catch is known as the reverse cup (figure 7.6, *a-c*). Instead of putting your hands together with the fingers pointing away from you and your little fingers touching, bend your elbows and raise your hands with your fingers pointing towards you and your thumbs touching. You might find it easier to relax your hands in this position as you watch the ball right into them. You still allow the elbows to give in order to cushion the ball to your chest. Either method can achieve a high percentage of success, but try both in practice to find out which you prefer.

Figure 7.6   Reverse Cup

GET INTO POSITION

1. Move quickly to get into position directly under falling ball
2. Hold hands higher than eyes
3. Point fingers back towards you
4. Touch thumbs

a

MAKE THE CATCH

1. Catch ball in stronger hand

b

GIVE WITH BALL

1. Allow arms and hands to give with ball
2. Allow ball to come to rest on right shoulder

c

Flat Catches

When a catch is hit hard at you on a flat trajectory, you have little time to get into position; however, you still need to give yourself the best possible chance of catching it. If the ball reaches you below chest height, your fingers should be pointing down with your head directly in line with the ball. Watch the ball right into your hands and allow your elbows to give (figure 7.7), just as you did with a high catch.

Figure 7.7	Catching a Flat Ball Below Chest Height

MAKE THE CATCH

1. Get behind line of ball
2. Prepare to receive ball at waist height
3. Hold hands in position to catch ball
4. Keep little fingers butted together
5. Point fingers down
6. Watch ball into hands
7. Allow elbows to give as with high catch

If the ball arrives above chest height, reverse your hands so that your thumbs are together and your fingers are pointing upwards (figure 7.8). Remember the join of your hands is the weakest point of the cup you fashion, so try to take the ball in your strongest hand. This is especially important if the ball is travelling at speed directly at your head. Although getting your head in the correct position and watching the ball intently help you to judge the line, turn your head to one side as you take the catch in case the ball bursts through your hands and goes into your face. With practice, you will become adept at turning your head as your hands give with the ball and let it come to rest on your shoulder.

Figure 7.8   Catching a Flat Ball Above Chest Height

MAKE THE CATCH

1. Judge ball's line
2. Hold hands in position to catch ball in front of face
3. Point fingers upwards
4. Butt thumbs together
5. Turn head out of way as you catch ball
6. Give with hands
7. Let hands with ball come to rest on shoulder

Misstep
When the ball is hit hard in the air to you at head height, you get your hands on it, but it then pops out.

Correction
As with all catches, you need to relax your hands as you catch the ball. You would do so if you were catching an egg, so apply the same principle with a cricket ball.

Catches Close to the Wicket

Most commonly, catches are taken close to the wicket. Whether in the slips, at short leg or silly point, these are often reaction catches; once again, good technique will improve your chances of making these catches. If you are standing back in the slips with a fast bowler operating, technique is all-important because these are not really reaction catches. At first slip, you can watch the ball all the way from the bowler's hand and have time to react. If you are further around in the slip cordon and in the gully, you might find it easier to watch the outside edge of the bat.

When in the slips, crouch down with your feet comfortably apart and ready to move in either direction (figure 7.9a). Some slip fielders put their weight on the insides of both feet; doing so makes it easier to push off in either direction. Your weight should always be on the balls of your feet rather than on the heels. Your hands are low in the ready position because you have back muscles designed to lift your body up. Your hands are ready to take the catch; your head is still. Never allow your fingers to point at the ball, no matter what type of catch you are making, or you will be particularly vulnerable to a finger injury.

Misstep

When fielding in the slips, you find yourself reaching down for slip catches that often end up on the ground.

Correction

You are either getting up too quickly or not getting low enough in the first place.

Figure 7.9   Catch Close to Wicket

CROUCH

1. Get into position to take catch
2. Keep eyes parallel to ground
3. Keep hands ready to take ball
4. Bend knees to get body close to ground
5. Stand with feet comfortably apart
6. Keep weight on inside of balls of feet, not back on heels

a

(continued)

Figure 7.9 (continued)

MOVE TO ONE SIDE

1. Push off inside of left foot if ball is to the right
2. Hold hands in position to catch ball
3. Keep palms at right angles to ball's line of flight to prevent injury to ends of fingers
4. If ball goes wide, dive and perhaps take catch with one hand
5. Watch ball into hands
6. Take catch slightly in front of body if possible

b

As the ball comes, you will probably have to move right or left. If the ball comes straight at you, apply the same principles as for the hard, flat catch. If you do move to one side, keep watching the ball as closely as possible as it comes right into your hands or hand (figure 7.9b).

If you dive to take a catch, make sure you land properly. There is nothing more annoying than to dive and take a stunning catch, only to have the ball jarred out of your hand as your elbow hits the ground. Review step 8 on wicket-keeping to learn how to dive in the correct manner.

It is vital that your hands do not become tense in the slips. Hard hands usually mean hard luck for the fielder, good luck for the batsman. It is the same when fielding close to the bat, square of or in front of the wicket. All the same principles apply, but a high proportion of catches that come your way in these positions will be of the bat or pad variety rather than straight edges. You have to be ready to dive forwards as well as sideways, and you should also be ready for a catch off the face of the bat. You need to apply all the principles mentioned earlier. Above all, keep your fingers from pointing at the ball.

Misstep
Your reaction time is slow when fielding close to the bat.

Correction
Unless you are fielding at first slip, where you watch the ball from the bowler's hand, try watching the edge of the bat rather than the ball.

You also need to keep watching the ball very closely. You will not be able to watch it from the bowler's hand, so you need sharp reactions to respond as soon as you see the ball coming close enough to be within your grasp. You also need physical courage, especially at short leg, where the ball can fly in your direction with only

a millisecond for you to decide whether to opt for attempting the catch or for self-preservation. The advent of helmets, shin pads and boxes for close fielders has alleviated the dangers, but short leg is not known as Boot Hill (after the graveyard in Dodge City beloved of westerns) for nothing.

Catching Drill 1. *High Catches*

Have a feeder hit high balls towards you. It doesn't matter how far away the feeder is. Make high catches. Attempt six catches.

To Increase Difficulty

- Have the feeder hit the ball higher and on different trajectories and lines.

To Decrease Difficulty

- Have the feeder hit the ball straight toward you and not as high.

Success Check

- Judge the trajectory before moving.

- After judging the trajectory, get into position to take the catch with either a conventional or reverse cup.
- Try to take the catch with your hands above eye level.
- Allow your hands and arms to give as you catch the ball.

Score Your Success

5 or 6 catches = 5 points

3 or 4 catches = 3 points

1 or 2 catches = 1 point

Your Score ___

Catching Drill 2. *Head-Height Catches*

Have a feeder hit hard balls to you at about head height from about 10 yards (9.1 m) away. Catch the ball at head height. Attempt six catches.

To Increase Difficulty

- Have the feeder hit the ball harder and to the side instead of straight toward you.

To Decrease Difficulty

- Have the feeder hit the ball straight toward you and not so hard.

Success Check

- Get your hands directly behind the line of the ball, with your fingers pointing up.

- Watch the ball right into your hands, but take your head out of the line as the ball reaches your hands.
- Allow your hands to give as you catch the ball, taking it one side of your head or the other and letting it rest on your shoulder.

Score Your Success

5 or 6 catches = 5 points

3 or 4 catches = 3 points

1 or 2 catches = 1 point

Your Score ___

Catching Drill 3.   *Catches in the Slips*

Have a feeder throw the ball hard at shoulder height toward a batsman. The batsman deflects a catch towards you in the slips. Attempt six catches.

To Increase Difficulty

- The batsman can hit the ball harder and at different heights, forcing you to move one way or the other.

To Decrease Difficulty

- The batsman does not hit the ball as hard and hits it straight toward you.

Success Check

- Take up a position with your hands close to the ground, knees flexed, weight on the balls of your feet and eyes parallel to the ground.

- Watch the ball into your hands, which should always be pointing at right angles to the line of the ball.
- Take the catch in two hands if possible, allowing them to give as you take the catch.

Score Your Success

5 or 6 catches = 5 points

3 or 4 catches = 3 points

1 or 2 catches = 1 point

Your Score ____

Catching Drill 4.   *Short-Leg Catches*

A feeder lobs the ball to a batsman. The batsman hits balls to you fielding at short leg. Attempt six catches.

To Increase Difficulty

- The batsman can hit the ball harder and to the side instead of straight toward you.

To Decrease Difficulty

- The batsman does not hit the ball as hard and hits it straight toward you.

Success Check

- Crouch down and watch the bat in order to pick up the flight of the ball.

- Watch the ball right into your hands.
- Allow your hands to give as you catch the ball.

Score Your Success

5 or 6 catches = 5 points

3 or 4 catches = 3 points

1 or 2 catches = 1 point

Your Score ____

THROWING

It was not long ago that some fielders were noted for having good throws, while others were picked out as candidates for the 'one for the throw' school of fielding. Currently, at the top level at least, all fielders must be able to deliver hard, accurate throws from anywhere in the outfield. When such fielders were rare, they were known as having strong arms, but as the standard of throwing has risen, so has the understanding of what action produces a good throw. It is not just a strong arm but also a strong technique that produces those bullet-like throws that whistle into the wicket-keeper's gloves alongside the bails.

The grip used by a bowler always gets a lot of attention, but a fielder also needs to adjust his grip on the ball before throwing it. As you field the ball, manoeuvre it in your hand so that the seam is at right angles to the line of the throw (figure 7.10). This prevents the ball from swinging off target as it flies through the air. Some claim the ball will actually travel farther because the backward rotation imparted on release causes it to float in the air longer. It is worth spending a fraction of a second to get the grip right as you balance in order to achieve that flat, straight throw you are seeking.

With the ball in your hand, establish a strong base with your feet. This is where the power comes from. Get side-on to the target (figure 7.11a), which can involve taking a step towards the target to give yourself some bodily momen-

tum in the right direction. As you do so, point at the target with your non-throwing hand or elbow, then draw your throwing hand up behind you. You want to ensure that at the moment of release the elbow on your throwing arm is not below the level of your shoulder. If it drops, you increase the chances of injuring your shoulder because of rotation in the joint.

Figure 7.10 Seam is at right angles to the line of the throw.

Misstep
You can throw the ball a long way, but it is not always in the right direction.

Correction
Check that you are side-on to the target and point at it with your front arm or elbow. Also check that you are turning the seam in your hand as you pick the ball up so that the seam will not cause the ball to swing as it travels through the air.

What follows is like a spring uncoiling. Your hips start the movement, becoming square to the target rather than sideways. The torso follows, and as your front arm pulls back tight in to your body, your shoulders turn square to the target (figure 7.11b), and your throwing arm whips through to send the ball on its unerring

way (figure 7.11c). All this is completed in a flash, but it is important to include all the elements of a good throw in the sequence. The set-up is vital, and those seconds you take to get the grip right and the base established is time well spent in order to achieve consistent success.

Figure 7.11   **Throwing the Ball**

ESTABLISH A STRONG BASE

1. Stand in side-on position with feet spread
2. Point non-throwing arm or elbow at target
3. Draw back throwing arm ready to throw

a

SQUARE BODY TO TARGET

1. Hips, torso and shoulders uncoil in that order to produce maximum leverage

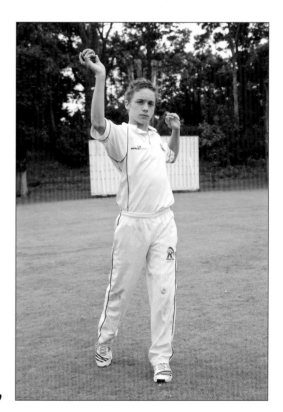

b

THROW BALL

1. Hips, torso and shoulders uncoil in direction of target

2. Throwing arm is last part of body to strike through

3. Ball is released at target

c

Misstep

However hard you try to throw the ball, there is no power to it.

Correction

Make sure you adopt a good throwing technique, which will enable you to throw more powerfully.

Throwing Drill. *Flat Throws*

Have a feeder hit balls along the ground to you. Begin with a distance of about 25 yards (23.9 m). Pick up each ball and return it accurately to the wicket-keeper with a hard, flat throw. Attempt six throws.

If a feeder and wicket-keeper are unavailable, perform the drill on your own. Mark a target on a wall. Throw the ball at the target and collect the rebound. If you decide on this option, use a tennis or rubber ball.

To Increase Difficulty

- Increase the length of the throw by moving farther away from the target.
- If you are performing the drill on your own, reduce the size of the target.

To Decrease Difficulty

- Decrease the length of the throw by moving closer to the target.
- If you are performing the drill on your own, increase the size of the target.

Success Check

- Stop the ball and adjust the seam as you prepare to throw; it should be at right angles to the direction of the throw and in your fingers.
- Get side-on to the target with your weight on your back foot and either your front arm or elbow pointing at the target.
- Draw your throwing arm back with the ball above shoulder height to prevent putting too much strain on that shoulder as it rotates during the throw.
- Start to unwind the hips, torso and shoulders as you transfer your weight forward, releasing the ball at the end of the unwinding process.

Score Your Success

5 or 6 throws reach the target on the full (on the fly) = 5 points

3 or 4 throws reach the target on the full (on the fly) = 3 points

1 or 2 throws reach the target on the full (on the fly) = 1 point

Your Score ___

Fielding Drill. *All-Around Fielding*

Get out on a field with a wicket-keeper and bowler positioned at the relevant ends of the pitch. Have the coach or a teammate stand at the striker's end and hit a variety of catches: balls along the ground to be intercepted and balls that go past you for you to chase and retrieve and then return to a called end.

To Increase Difficulty

- Extend the range of throws that have to be made.
- Have balls for a particular skill either harder or higher.

To Decrease Difficulty

- Have the feeder ensure that the throws will be over a shorter distance

- Have balls hit more softly or not as high.

Success Check

- Refer to the relevant section of the previous text to make sure you have a good technique for each skill.

Score Your Success

5 or 6 successful techniques = 5 points

3 or 4 successful techniques = 3 points

1 or 2 successful techniques = 1 point

Your Score _____

SUCCESS SUMMARY OF FIELDING

Much of fielding is about confidence. Increase your confidence to deal successfully with fielding challenges by making sure your technique for each skill is good. Judge where the ball is going as early as possible and then move to it as quickly as possible. Get your feet, head and hands in the correct position to perform the fielding skill as needed, and make sure your throw is fast and accurate. The important thing is not to panic, and make sure your technique will stand up to performance under pressure. It is all very well to take high catches when there is no pressure; the important thing is to be able to hold such a catch when it comes off the last ball of a match, and the result depends on you holding it. Practice diligently. Your skill level will increase, and you will have the confidence that breeds success.

Before moving on to step 8, Wicket-Keeping, evaluate how you did on the fielding drills in this step. Tally your scores to determine how well you have mastered the skill of fielding. If you scored 50 points, you are ready to move on to step 8. If you did not score 50 points, practise the drills again until you raise your scores before moving on to step 8.

Intercept Drills

1. Long-Barrier Intercepts ___ out of 5

2. Two-Handed Intercepts ___ out of 5

3. One-Handed Intercepts ___ out of 5

4. Mixed Intercepts ___ out of 5

Retrieving Drills

1. Chase and Retrieve ___ out of 5

2. Chase and Return to Called End ___ out of 5

Catching Drills

1. High Catches ___ out of 5

2. Head-Height Catches ___ out of 5

3. Catches in the Slips ___ out of 5

4. Short-Leg Catches ___ out of 5

Throwing Drill

1. Flat Throws ___ out of 5

Fielding Drill

1. All-Around Fielding ___ out of 5

Total ___ *out of 60*

This fielding step frequently mentioned the wicket-keeper, the natural target for fielding throws. The wicket-keeper is a very important member of the side, for he tends to be involved in every ball bowled. He either takes the ball if it goes past the bat or is ready to take the throw. Wicket-keeping is a demanding role, but it is one that gives great satisfaction when performed well. It is also a role that is often performed by one of the most accomplished fielders in a side, one who has good eye–hand co-ordination. If you have done well in this step, you might consider applying those skills to wicket-keeping.

Wicket-Keeping

The wicket-keeper is the heartbeat of a side, the pivotal point of the whole fielding effort. A poor wicket-keeper prevents any team from reaching its potential because he sets the tone. Conversely, a good glove man can lift the performance of the whole side by supporting the bowlers with appeals, tidying up poor returns from fielders and, of course, catching every chance that comes his way and not letting anything else past him.

A good wicket-keeper is agile, fit and able to concentrate for long periods. He is a constant source of encouragement to his team-mates as the ball virtually melts into his gloves whenever he takes it. It is unusual for a wicket-keeper to be hopeless with the bat; indeed, he is expected to make a significant contribution to the scorecard. One of the game's eternal debates concerns whether selectors should pick their very best wicket-keeper, irrespective of his batting ability, or settle for lesser ability with the gloves in favour of someone who might produce more runs. There is no doubting that runs from the wicket-keeper are useful, but do they outweigh the risk of dropping a catch offered early by the opposition's star batsman?

The true test of a wicket-keeper comes when he is standing up to the wicket. Most proficient fielders can make a passable impression of the role when standing back, ready to take the ball from a quicker bowler, for there is little difference between doing that and fielding at slip. But when he is standing up, the wicket-keeper's job becomes a vocation. Courage comes into the equation as well as talent, for when the bat is flailing, the ball is turning and lifting or the ball is being delivered by medium pacers, a flying bail or edged ball can cause serious injury.

The wicket-keeper also is in the best position to see what the ball is doing, feel how hard it hits his gloves and assess how the batsmen are coping with particular bowlers. Often, he is the captain's first lieutenant if he does not assume the captain's role himself. Either way, he is a very influential member of the team and often is something of a character. He can have a direct input on the outcome of a match through catches, stumpings and general performance. You should judge a wicket-keeper not by the number of dismissals he makes, but by the ratio of chances he takes to those he does not.

POSITIONING

Another of cricket's debates concerns whether wicket-keepers should stand back or up to the stumps, especially with the medium pacers. When a wicket-keeper stands up to anyone above medium pace, it certainly gives cause for comment as this is the true test of his ability. But he does not just stand anywhere he fancies, whether up or back. Numerous factors come into play, even when he is standing back, and his job is rather more straightforward.

As a wicket-keeper, you want to make sure the ball reaches you at thigh height when you are standing back (figure 8.1, *a* and *b*). Any lower and edges probably will not carry to you. You would not be comfortable continually taking the ball much higher than that when a higher bounce or a top edge will take the ball over your head. You also want to be in a position to see the ball all the way from the bowler's hand, which is just to the off side of the stumps. This positioning should ensure that you take a vast majority of balls with minimal movement.

a

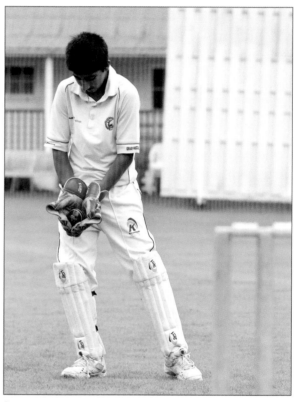

b

Figure 8.1 *(a)* Wicket-keeper's stance when standing back, which gives him a good view of the ball all the way from the bowler's hand. *(b)* Wicket-keeper takes the ball at thigh height.

Misstep
The ball hardly ever comes to you at the right height.

Correction
If you are standing back, your positioning is wrong. If you are standing up to the wicket, you might be getting up too early. Allow your gloves to rise with the bounce of the ball.

Some wicket-keepers appear to the uninformed observer to be better than others because they are forever diving about and making their takes look spectacular. In fact, the unspectacular wicket-keeper usually is more proficient because he uses his feet to get into position without needing to dive. Of course, when the good wicket-keeper reaches the end of his range

of footwork, he must dive, but only then. A top wicket-keeper will spend little time prone on the ground. With consistent bowlers in operation, he will allow for late movement. With an out-swing bowler, the wicket-keeper tries to take balls that come straight through just inside his body. If a ball takes an outside edge, he will have less ground to cover before taking the catch.

Misstep

You frequently have to dive to take the ball when it is not directed at the stumps.

Correction

Use footwork to get to the ball rather than diving unless the ball is at the outer limits of your range.

Standing up to the wicket (figure 8.2, *a* and *b*) creates the possibility of a stumping. You are still there to take catches and generally stop the ball, but the batsmen is put under additional pressure, knowing that he must keep one foot behind the line at all times if he is not to be dismissed. Meanwhile, you must ensure that the

stumps are within reach. You do not want to take the ball and then have to move forward before removing the bails. You also should watch the ball from the bowler's hand. For a right-handed batsman, your left foot will be on the line of the middle and off stumps.

a

b

Figure 8.2 Wicket-keeper standing up to the wicket. Weight is on the balls of the feet, gloves are together and ready to rise with the ball. Wicket-keeper still has a good view of the ball. *(a)* Front view; *(b)* side view.

The movement of the wicket-keeper's feet when standing up is determined by the line and bounce of the ball. You may not take the ball cleanly if you get up from your squatting position before seeing how the ball has bounced, which may cause you to hurriedly jab down on the ball with your gloves. It is important to keep your gloves down and only rise with the bounce, although you can straighten your legs earlier in case you have to move to the side. If the ball has not bounced much but is outside the off-stump, move your right foot parallel to the bowling crease so that you can get your head right over the line.

If the ball bounces more, perhaps reaching you above waist height, move your right foot across, but this time backwards at an angle of approximately 45 degrees to the crease (figure 8.3). This will enable you to get your body out of the way as you take the rising ball with your hands moving up and backwards. You also will keep your right foot out of the way of any edge that you cannot take but which would carry to slip.

Figure 8.3   Wicket-keeper catching the ball above waist height.

Misstep
When the ball bounces outside off-stump, you have difficulty getting your gloves up to take it.

Correction
Make sure your right foot moves backwards at 45 degrees to the stumps, thereby getting you body out of the way and allowing room for your gloves to rise with the ball.

CATCHING

As a wicket-keeper, your positioning and movement determine how many catching opportunities come within your reach, but once you have a glove or gloves on the ball, you want to make sure it sticks. Watch the ball right into your gloves; keep your fingers pointing at right angles to the line of the ball (figure 8.4) so there is no danger of being hit on the ends of your fingers. As you take the catch, your gloves should give to cradle the ball into safe keeping. Only when it is firmly lodged in your hands should you appeal or hurl the ball skywards in celebration.

Figure 8.4   Wicket-Keeper Catching

1. Follow ball with eyes right into gloves
2. Use gloves to form large cup for ball to nestle into

This is fine when the ball comes to you comfortably within your grasp. However, when you are forced to dive, it is important to land the correct way to prevent the ball from popping out of your gloves as your elbows hit the ground. If you dive for a one-handed catch to your right (figure 8.5), scoop up the ball with your right hand; once the ball is safely in your glove, twist your body so that you land on the back of your right shoulder. For a two-handed catch to your right (figure 8.6), let the ball come into your gloves and then twist to land on the back of your left shoulder. This might appear complicated, but it should become simple with practice and will produce improved results.

Figure 8.5   One-Handed Diving Catch

1. Dive towards the ball
2. Watch ball into glove
3. Secure catch
4. Twist to land on back of shoulder
5. Scoop ball so it will not be jarred out on impact with ground

Figure 8.6   Two-Handed Diving Catch

1. Dive towards the ball
2. Watch ball into glove
3. Secure catch
4. Turn in air to land on back of shoulder
5. Prevent ball from being jarred out on impact with ground

Misstep
The ball pops out of your grasp when you dive for a catch.

Correction
Make sure you land correctly. Do not land on your elbow but twist after you take the catch to land on the back of your shoulder. If you are moving to your right, land on the back of your right shoulder for a one-handed catch and the back of your left shoulder for a two-handed catch.

STUMPING

Stumping marks a quality wicket-keeper. The batsman plays and misses while shifting his foot a hair's breadth out of his ground. In a flash, the wicket-keeper takes the ball and whips off the bails, and another wicket has fallen. Such success demands a high level of concentration and composure. If the wicket-keeper gets too excited about a stumping opportunity, he will almost certainly miss it.

The ball has to pass the stumps before you are permitted to touch it, provided it has not come off the bat or the batsman. That is where the composure comes in: do not grab at the ball as soon as you realise there is a chance. Get your gloves into position, allow the ball to come to you and only then move your hands towards the bails (figure 8.7, *a* and *b*). Until you hold the ball, stumping is not on the agenda.

Figure 8.7 | **Stumping**

GATHER BALL

1. Gather ball once it passes stumps
2. Lean head and body towards wicket

a

REMOVE BAILS

1. Take off bails before batsman can regain his ground

b

Misstep
When going for a stumping, you frequently drop the ball.

Correction
You are snatching at the ball rather than watching the ball right into your gloves before taking them to the bails.

It was noted earlier that when you stand up to the wicket, you should always be able to reach the bails from where you take the ball. That applies to the distance you stand back behind the stumps, but the width of the ball determines how far wide of the stumps you must go. Even so, you can help yourself by leaning in towards the stumps as you begin to bring the ball back to the bails. Even when the ball is wide of leg stump, watch its line and trajectory for as long as possible before it is hidden by the batsman's body. Then step across to the leg side as the ball reappears, watch it into your gloves and, leaning into the stumps, whip the bails off. That is a classical piece of wicket-keeping!

RUN-OUTS

More often than not, you effect a run-out. A run-out may follow a remarkable piece of fielding and return towards the stumps. Without your help, though, the fielder's excellent work will probably come to nothing. If you are standing up, get into position to take the return. However, if you are standing back, as soon as you see the batsman hit the ball, set off to get alongside the stumps as quickly as possible. Be alert to the situation. If you think you have the best chance of effecting a run-out, demand that the ball be thrown to your end.

As the ball arrives, apply the same principles as you would for a stumping. Watch the ball right into your gloves, lean your body towards the stumps and take the ball back to break the wicket as quickly as you can. Sometimes the throw will be wayward, resulting in a considerable distance to take the ball back to the stumps. That is where agility comes in. The most difficult return to take is one that comes in on the half volley. In this case, try to get behind the line of the ball and lead with your head in the same way as a batsman starting to drive (figure 8.8). Instead of the bat being on the ball just as it hits the ground, your gloves should be there to collect the ball and take it to the stumps.

Figure 8.8 Wicket-keeper securing a half-volley return.

There is one other common way for you to effect a run-out: when the ball is returned to you and you realise there is more chance of a dismissal at the bowler's end. As the ball arrives, remove your glove from your throwing hand and take the ball in your other glove; transfer the ball into your throwing hand for a shy at the stumps at the other end or a throw to the bowler (figure 8.9). This decision requires awareness of the situation and the whereabouts of the stumps at the other end. And you also need to bear in mind that you might be facing in any direction when you receive the ball. That is all part of the wicket-keeper's demanding, yet thoroughly satisfying job.

Figure 8.9　Throwing the Ball to the Bowler

PREPARATION

1. Remove glove from throwing hand
2. Transfer ball to throwing hand
3. Throw ball to bowler

Wicket-Keeping Drill 1. *Behind the Stumps*

Stand behind the stumps. Have a feeder serve the ball from just short of a pitch length away for you to take and return to the top of the stumps. Take six balls.

To Increase Difficulty

- Have the feeder serve the ball faster, without telling you whether the ball is going to be straight, to the leg or to the off.

To Decrease Difficulty

- The feeder lets you know the direction of the delivery before he releases the ball.

Success Check

- Take the correct position so you can see the ball all the way.
- Only raise your gloves with the bounce of the ball.

- Watch the ball right into your gloves, holding them at right angles to the line of the ball, before taking them back to the top of the stumps.
- If the ball is wide of the stumps, move one foot (.3 m) parallel to the crease if the ball is not bouncing; move your foot back at 45 degrees to the crease if the ball is bouncing high.

Score Your Success

5 or 6 successful takes = 5 points

3 or 4 successful takes = 3 points

1 or 2 successful takes = 1 point

Your Score ___

Wicket-Keeping Drill 2. *Stand Back*

Stand back from the stumps and have a feeder serve the ball from just short of a pitch length away for you to take. Take six balls.

To Increase Difficulty

- Have a batsman give catches and mix up straight, leg and off-side deliveries.

To Decrease Difficulty

- Have the feeder call out the direction of the delivery before releasing the ball.
- Do not use a batsman.

Success Check

- Take up the correct position so you can see the ball all the way; make sure it arrives at thigh height.

- Watch the ball right into your gloves, holding them at right angles to the line of the ball.
- If the ball is wide of the stumps, move your feet to get as close to the ball as possible. Dive only if the ball is outside that range.
- Should you need to dive, twist in the air after you have taken the ball to land on the back of the correct shoulder rather than your elbows so that the ball will not pop out.

Score Your Success

5 or 6 successful takes = 5 points

3 or 4 successful takes = 3 points

1 or 2 successful takes = 1 point

Your Score ___

Wicket-Keeping Drill 3. *Diving*

Put down crash mats to your right and left. Have a feeder stand about 5 yards (4.6 m) away and serve six balls to your right and left so that you have to dive to catch the ball.

To Increase Difficulty

- Do not have the feeder tell you to which side the catch is going. You will need to make the decision and show good technique in catching the ball and landing correctly.
- Have the feeder serve the ball quicker and wider.

To Decrease Difficulty

- The feeder tells you the direction of the catch before he releases the ball.
- Have the feeder slow down the delivery and not throw the balls as wide.

Success Check

- Take up the correct position so you can see the ball and move easily in either direction.
- Watch the ball into your gloves; always keep your gloves at right angles to the line of the ball.
- As you dive, twist in the air after you have taken the ball to land on the back of the correct shoulder rather than your elbows so that the ball will not pop out.

Score Your Success

5 or 6 successful takes (catches) = 5 points

3 or 4 successful takes (catches) = 3 points

1 or 2 successful takes (catches) = 1 point

Your Score ___

Wicket-Keeping Drill 4. *Match Situation*

Have a bowler deliver six balls as in a match situation and have a batsman deliberately miss a high proportion of the deliveries. Mix up straight, leg and off-side deliveries. Put crash mats down if you are standing back from the wickets to practice diving for wide balls. Both batsman and bowler should realise that this drill is designed with you in mind, not either of them.

To Increase Difficulty

- Stand up to the stumps against a medium-pace bowler.

To Decrease Difficulty

- Stand back from the stumps against a medium-pace bowler.

Success Check

- Take up the correct position so you can see the ball all the way; make sure it arrives at thigh height.

- Watch the ball right into your gloves; always keep you gloves at right angles to the line of the ball.
- If the ball is wide of the stumps, move your feet to get as close to the ball as possible. You will only need to dive if the ball is outside that range.
- Should you need to dive, twist in the air after you have taken the ball to land on the back of the correct shoulder rather than your elbows so that the ball will not pop out.

Score Your Success

5 or 6 successful takes = 5 points

3 or 4 successful takes = 3 points

1 or 2 successful takes = 1 point

Your Score ___

SUCCESS SUMMARY OF WICKET-KEEPING

The wicket-keeper plays a crucial part in overall team performance. As a wicket-keeper, you set the tone for the fielding side, so it is vital for you to be physically fit to withstand the rigours of the job. You need to have a passion about keeping wicket. And you need to retain your enthusiasm all the time your side is in the field because your vitality will rub off on others.

Some people are natural wicket-keepers; others might not be as gifted but still reach an acceptable standard. Either way, it is those wicket-keepers who work at their games who have the greatest success. Wicket-keepers need to apply the basic techniques as described in this step; once those are mastered, successful wicket-keepers continue to work so that their standard improves all the time. Like every other aspect of the game, the best wicket-keepers are those who do the simple things better than anyone else.

Before moving on to step 9, Team Roles, evaluate how you did on the wicket-keeping drills in this step. Tally your scores to determine how well you have mastered the skill of wicket-keeping. If you scored 15 points, you are ready to move on to step 9. If you did not score 15 points, practice the drills again until you raise your scores before moving on to step 9

Wicket-Keeping Drills

1. Behind the Stumps _____ out of 5
2. Stand Back _____ out of 5
3. Diving _____ out of 5
4. Match Situation _____ out of 5

Total _____ **out of 20**

Now it is time to move on to see how the wicket-keeper fits in with the team ethos and look at the roles other players perform. The interaction between members of a side can make a team perform better than its individual components might suggest. It is a wonderful feeling to be part of such a team.

Team Roles

One of the great things about cricket that it provides a role for everyone, no matter how tall or short, fat or thin. There is nothing more fascinating than watching a strapping fast bowler being defied by a diminutive batsman who can cancel out the physical disparity by the application of correct cricketing skills. Conversely, you may see a powerful batsman being tied up in knots by a clever spin bowler. The game's appeal rests on a balance between bat and ball; if ever one of the two takes precedence, the character of the game is lost until that balance is restored.

The presence of so many facets in the game encourages a wide range of abilities. The ideal cricketer has a sound defence and an array of attacking strokes when batting, can bowl like the wind and spin the ball on glass and is so good in the field that he can catch sparrows. Alas, such players are rare, and to be outstanding in just one element or competent in at least two measures up well to requirements. It is this rich variety that gives the game its soul.

It must always be remembered that cricket is a team game, and that the players are members of a single team. If that team is to be successful, all the parts have to function as a unit, with batsmen scoring runs, bowlers taking wickets and the wicket-keeper and fielders playing their

roles. Should individual ambition become more important than the team ethic or should factions develop within the side, there is little chance of a team forming a winning mentality. If there is a feeling of togetherness, there is every chance that the potential of the team will be realised.

If players are more interested in their team's performance than in their own, that joyous state exists where, to use that time-honoured expression, the whole is worth more than the sum of its parts. Players often go through three stages before they adopt that philosophy. When first selected for a side, they feel fulfilled they have reached their goal. That lasts for a few matches before they become consumed by the desire for good personal performances in order to remain in the team. Only after that will they subscribe to the idea that team performance is of paramount importance. They learn to accept and value the idea that even if they have failed to score runs or take wickets themselves, they can take pleasure in the fact that someone else has ensured the team's success.

This does not mean that personal performances are not important to the team effort. Success demands that everybody does his job well. When doubts arise about a player's ability to perform his given task, selection reflects those doubts. For instance, if there are concerns about the top-order batting, an extra batsman might be included at the expense of a bowler, or a lesser wicket-keeper might be selected because he is more likely to contribute with his bat. However, before players can fulfil their roles in the team, those roles have to be defined.

CAPTAIN

As well as performing his own specialist role, the captain needs to perform many others: leader, strategist, diplomat, psychologist, disciplinarian, motivator, communicator and agony aunt. It helps if he is lucky as well! Such are the demands on the captain that it is no surprise if his playing form dips. However, a player with true leadership qualities is more likely to be inspired by captaincy than to find the role oppressive. Being willing and able to undertake the role should go a long way towards gaining respect from other members of the team. Once a captain commands respect, he is a long way down the road to success.

Respect for the captain is enhanced by the way he conducts himself on and off the field and by the way he runs the side. The captain needs a thorough understanding of the game at the level he is playing. Players soon see through a captain who is ignorant of basic strategies, which will make it difficult for him to be a good manager. This does not mean the captain has to be forever coming up with wild and adventurous ideas for winning a game, but he should be able to make the most of the resources available to him. Anyone can be a successful captain if blessed with 10 world-class players in his side. It becomes rather more taxing if his players are no better than mediocre. There have been few great captains of poor sides.

A good captain will know which players need sympathy, cajoling and gentle persuasion, and which have to be challenged to perform. He will know the limitations and potential of his team in order to make sensible declarations. He must be a good reader of the game, quickly determining the strengths and weaknesses of the opposition and exploiting them by shrewd field placements and bowling changes.

This is not always as straightforward as it might appear. For example, a captain might well spot that a particular batsman is uncomfortable against pace. However, his main strike bowler

The team captain performs many roles both on and off the field.

has been bowling for six overs at full throttle. Does he rest that bowler to conserve his energies, or does he keep that bowler going to make the breakthrough when he might have nothing left for another spell later? There is no right or wrong answer. Other factors to be taken into account include the importance of the particular wicket, whether the bowler in question will be needed again if he can take it, the proximity of the lunch or tea interval and what other resources are available.

If a captain wants his players to put the team's interests before their own, he must do so as well. The time for a captain to drop down the order when his side is batting is not when the opposition have a fearsome attack, but when there are easy runs to be had. When in the field, the captain should take the ball when the pitch is flat and the batsmen are on the rampage, rather than when the others have done the hard yards, and he rolls over nine, ten and jack to grab the best figures.

A captain who puts himself at the heart of the action is not going to be questioned when he asks the same of his players. It might be that his bowler has four wickets and desperately wants a fifth. The match might be going very much in his side's favour, with many runs required and a new batsman at the non-striker's end, while an established batsman is facing the last ball of an over. In order to put the new batsman on strike for the next over, the bowler should be told to forego the chance of five-wicket glory for the moment with a ball that is unlikely to take a wicket but will ensure that a single is not scored. The captain sets the field to prevent that single, which might well result in the ball going for four, but runs are not as important as opening up an end. The bowler knows that the captain will do all he can to give him a new batsman to bowl at in future overs and therefore does as he is told. The ploy may or may not work, but it shows that the captain is thinking about the game.

In such a situation, a certain amount of luck will come into play, and it is luck that plays a vital role at the outset of a match. The two captains toss a coin to give one of them the choice of batting or bowling first. No amount of practice can help you with that unless you employ underhand tactics. The legendary Victorian cricketer W.G. Grace was not averse to gamesmanship, and whenever possible he would make sure the opposition captain used a penny for the toss. In those days, the queen's head was shown on one side and a depiction of Britannia on the other. While the coin was in the air, Grace would call, "The lady." Regardless of which side landed face up, he had called it correctly; he would then say whether he would bat or bowl first. Of course, you need to know what you are going to do if you win the toss, and that comes down to judgement rather than luck.

OPENING BATSMEN

The first job of the opening batsmen is to survive. They should have sound technique in order to do so and be even sounder temperamentally. By definition, they will be expected to go out and face the fastest of the opposition bowlers at their freshest and when the ball is new. It is not a job for the fainthearted, but good opening batsmen relish the challenge.

For the opening batsmen, this is a partnership; it is not two individuals playing on their own. The opening batsmen need to communicate and be ready to take any runs going in order

The opening batsmen must communicate effectively with each other in order to run between the wickets successfully.

to rotate the strike. This prevents the bowlers from settling down against a particular style of batsman and spreads the concentration workload. Not letting the bowlers settle is particularly important when a right- and left-handed opening pair is used. If the bowler continually has to change his line to attack a different type of batsman, it is harder for him to concentrate on his primary job of getting them out.

If the opening batsmen are going to run effectively between the wickets, they need good understanding between them. With regular opening partnerships, an almost intuitive understanding exists, and calling becomes virtually unnecessary. The customary calls of "Yes," "No" and "Wait" become redundant after a time. There are even cases, particularly in limited-overs cricket, in which the batsmen assume there is at least a single off every ball unless either of them calls otherwise.

This calling approach is only for a pair of batsmen who have absolute trust in each other. In general, the rule is that when the ball can be seen easily by the batsman on strike, he calls. Therefore, anywhere from backward point to mid-wicket is the striker's call. Anywhere else, it is the non-striker who calls. Calling should be clear and loud, and either batsman should have the right to veto a call to run if he is unable to

make it. This might happen if, unbeknown to his partner, the striker slips on playing a shot.

The non-striker should always back up as the bowler delivers the ball so he has less distance to run if he is required to do so. When running, each batsman should carry his bat in the hand that allows him to best see where the ball has gone. If a right-handed striker plays the ball into the covers and runs, he should carry his bat in his left hand in order to stretch for the crease at the other end and still be facing the direction of the ball. A right-handed non-striker in the same situation carries the bat in his right hand for the same reason. This will enable both batsmen to see if another run is available without craning their necks to look over their shoulders at the ball. If they are running more than a single, they will need to change hands as they do so to be in the correct position at the other end.

Batsmen should always make sure that they ground their bats over the popping crease (figure 9.1). Few things are worse than completing two or three runs and then having the umpire signal one short. And however hopeless the situation, give everything you have to make your ground. There have been many examples of a batsman giving up halfway down the pitch because he thinks he is going to be run-out, only to have the wicket-keeper or bowler drop the return. Had

Figure 9.1 The batsman grounds his bat and slides it over the popping crease.

the batsman gone for it and dived, he would have got in before the wicket had been broken.

Once the opening batsmen have become accustomed to the bowling and conditions, they can be a little more expansive in their stroke play. After having done all the hard work, they should not throw their wickets away; however, they do need to press on if they are going to capitalise on the start they have enjoyed. As they become more confident, they effectively become middle-order batsmen in the context of the game.

MIDDLE-ORDER BATSMEN

The key to a large total of runs is building partnerships. Unless the opening batsmen have put on a serious stand and the middle-order batsmen do not have to worry unduly about the loss of further wickets, they need to play themselves in before taking the bowlers on. There is an old saying in cricket that one brings two, meaning that if one wicket falls, another will follow. This is either because a member of a successful partnership loses concentration when his colleague is out and soon suffers the same fate or because a new batsman fails to play himself in properly and gets out.

Either way, it is a great fillip to the bowlers to break a big partnership, and they will be reinvigorated by a wicket. The bowlers then believe they can take another, and they frequently do. That is why a new batsman should take his time before launching into the shots that will speed him to a 50 or even a century. This is even more important if an early wicket falls. Any number three batsman should be able to gear his innings to the demands of the situation. He might need to think like an opening batsman if one of them was out very early, or he should be able to take the attack to the bowlers after a profitable opening partnership.

Should several wickets tumble early, batsmen four and five might be required to play the same way, but generally they are considered to be the best stroke makers in the order and the source of the bulk of the runs. Usually, they are classical batsmen with an enviable range of strokes. They should nonetheless play themselves in, setting themselves small targets rather than immediately thinking of a big score. They might discipline themselves not to attempt any attacking strokes, unless there is a rank bad ball, for the first three overs they are batting. They will pick up the odd run without having to play big strokes, so the next target might be double figures. They can then go up in increments of 10 until a major target such as 50 runs becomes the goal.

A batsman must never be satisfied with 50. He needs to go on to a really big score, well in excess of 100, before he can relax in the knowledge that his job is done. And even when he approaches that big personal tally, he needs to be aware of the pace at which he scores his runs. Often, there is talk of a one-paced batsman, meaning one who is unable to increase the tempo as he progresses. If he scores too slowly and fails to take a tiring attack apart, he will not be doing his best for the side.

At times, even the most fluent stroke maker has to curb his innate desire to attack and concentrate instead on preserving his wicket. If a win becomes impossible but a draw is still available, the chances of reaching safety are greatly enhanced if the middle-order batsmen can concentrate for long periods while runs are not flowing. They might prefer to cane the ball to all parts, but sometimes the needs of the team come before personal glory. That can be as difficult for someone who prefers to score quickly as it would be for a dour opening batsman to suddenly cut loose.

The situation may occur in which a middle-order batsman is left with only inferior batsmen in the closing stages of the innings. Such a situation requires special qualities, especially in terms of temperament. This batsman is responsible for protecting batsmen of lesser ability while scoring runs himself. It is not easy because captains will set fields to check his opportunities, and improvisation becomes essential to overcome restrictions. If 20 or 30 extra runs can be garnered by the tail with the help of the last remaining specialist batsman, he has done a job that may make the difference between victory and defeat.

ALL-ROUNDER

It is very easy to mistake a player who does not quite cut the mustard with either bat or ball for an all-rounder. He is not. That player is a bits and pieces cricketer who cannot command a place in the team as a specialist batsman or bowler but can do a bit of both. A genuine all-rounder can get into a team as either a batsman or a bowler; however, if he performs both roles in one match, that is a rare bonus. An all-rounder can make up for failure in one discipline by success in the other. As the sophistication of the game increases, though, there are fewer genuine all-rounders and more batsman who can bowl or bowlers who can chip in with useful runs.

It takes a special type of player to excel at more than one facet of the game. The practice needed to achieve competence in one is considerable, and that has to be doubled to reach the same level in both. That is why all-rounders tend to be gifted players who rely on natural ability rather than training to reach the top and stay there. The physical demands on an all-rounder are daunting. Unlike a pure batsman, an all-rounder cannot relax in the field, contemplating his next innings, nor can he put his feet up and relax when his side are batting, like an out-and-out bowler.

All-rounders come in several guises. All have to bat to earn the label, but some are quick bowlers or medium pacers, while others are spinners. The wicket-keeper/batsman all-rounder is becoming increasingly common, sadly at the expense of the genuine wicket-keeper. A wicket-keeper used to be selected for his ability with the gloves and might make a contribution with the bat. That balance has changed so that batsmen, especially fast-scoring batsmen, are taught to keep wicket. Just like the batsman/bowler all-rounder, a genuine wicket-keeper/batsman all-rounder is an asset to be cherished.

BOWLERS

The job of the bowlers is to take wickets. And keep the opposition batsmen from scoring. And do their share of fielding. Bowlers may also be called upon to determine the outcome of a match with their batting. The batsmen may take their side close to a target or to the safety of a draw, but then the bowlers may have to go out to finish the job. But unless they are all-rounders, their primary role is to win matches with the ball.

The attack is usually, but not always, opened by the quickest bowlers. Fast bowlers seldom rely exclusively on pace, but that is the weapon that earns them respect and their wickets at the top of the order when the ball is new. That is why they bowl to attacking fields, with wicket-keeper, slips, gully and short legs waiting to take the edges and deflections, rather than having men in front of the bat to protect the boundaries from drives. They do not intend to offer up half volleys, preferring to see the batsman on his back foot.

If the opening bowlers can knock over some top-order batsmen, they have started off well in fulfilling their role. They often will come back to polish off the tail or, in first-class cricket, return when the new ball becomes due. They form the spearhead of the attack, working to force a breach in the opposition defences that other bowlers can exploit or give themselves an opportunity to come back and take advantage of that initial breach.

Once the opening bowlers have had the chance to work on the ball and create a shiny and a rough side, the fast-medium or medium-pace bowlers take over. Because they bowl with less speed, the ball is in the air longer and has more chance to swing or deviate off the pitch if it lands on the still-prominent seam. These are the bowlers who deliver subtle variations, which are designed to deceive the batsman rather than blast him out. Like all bowlers, the medium pacers are expected to take wickets, but they should also make it difficult for the opposition to score. Without so much pace on the ball, the batsmen cannot rely on deflections to pick up runs. When batsmen have to go after the bowling, they take more chances.

Once the ball has become older and less suitable for quick bowling, the spinners come into the attack. Wrist spinners tend to give away more runs, but they are more potent. Finger spinners are likely to impose more control but often have to work harder for their wickets. Some captains underestimate the value of good spinners in their side and fail to utilise their talents properly. Batsmen may not feel the same physical apprehension against spin as they do against pace, but the mental torture a good spinner can exert makes him a very useful member of the attack, especially against good batsmen who can counter the physical challenge of pace. It is the same when the pitch begins to wear, and the spinners can extract more purchase, turn and unpredictable bounce from the surface.

Spinners also are needed if the pitch is flat, and the faster bowlers are not threatening. That is why it is important for any side to have a balanced attack. Attacks that are too reliant on pace often find playing conditions less favourable than expected, leaving the captain in a situation in which he can change the bowlers but not the bowling. That poses few questions for the batsmen to answer. One of the joys of cricket is that it can accommodate players with a variety of styles. Cricket comes into its own when this rich variety is on display for all to see.

Team Roles Drill 1. *Hit to the Marked Zone*

A batsman has to hit the ball into a marked area, irrespective of the line and length of the ball. The bowler can use a coloured ball that he conceals from the batsman before he bowls it. The batsman then has to hit the ball into a zone marked by coloured cones that coincide with the colour of the ball. The size and distance of the zones can be adjusted according to the space available. If a supply of coloured balls is unavailable, the coach can call out a coloured zone into which the ball must be hit as the bowler releases the ball. Each bowler faces six balls.

To Increase Difficulty

- Reduce the size of the zones.
- Call the zone that is the target later in the play and for a particular delivery.

To Decrease Difficulty

- Increase the size of the target zones.
- Inform the batsman early into which zone he must hit the ball.

Success Check

- Make sure you have a good set-up, with attention paid to grip, stance and backlift.
- Be aware of where the zones are so you can react quickly to the ball.
- Maintain good technique when playing the appropriate stroke.
- When an appropriate orthodox stroke cannot be played, adapt an orthodox stroke to meet the requirements of the situation.

Score Your Success

Play 5 or 6 balls into the correct zone = 5 points

Play 3 or 4 balls into the correct zone = 3 points

Play 1 or 2 balls into the correct zone = 1 point

Your Score ___

Team Roles Drill 2. *Quick Running*

A pair of batsmen face six balls from a bowler with fielders set back. On an outside field, fielders should be positioned 30 yards (27.4 m) from the bat. When practicing indoors, fielders should be touching the walls as the ball is delivered. Every time a batsman makes contact with the ball, both batsmen should complete a run, irrespective of where the ball goes.

To Increase Difficulty

- Allow the fielders to come closer to the bat.

To Decrease Difficulty

- Position the fielders farther away from the bat.

Success Check

- The batsman facing the bowler must have a good set-up.

- The non-striking batsman must back up and be ready to run.
- The facing batsman must try to work the ball into areas away from the fielders and be ready to run at all times.
- Both batsmen must run quickly and run their bats in correctly.

Score Your Success

Successfully complete 5 or 6 runs = 5 points

Successfully complete 3 or 4 runs = 3 points

Successfully complete 1 or 2 runs = 1 point

Your Score ___

Although the two drills in this step focus on the batsman, the bowler in these drills also can check how successful he is. The bowler can try to stop the batsman by bowling the ball on a line and length that makes it difficult for the batsman to hit the identified zone in drill 1. For drill 2, the bowler should try to bowl yorkers and slower balls to make it difficult for the batsman; the bowler follows through to prevent a run if the batsman simply stops the ball and runs. The bowler can score his success by reversing the batsman's score. For example, if the batsman successfully completes only one or two runs in six balls, the bowler scores 5 points, and so on. Fielders also can score on the same lines or the team can be scored collectively, whether batting or fielding.

SUCCESS SUMMARY OF TEAM ROLES

Tally your drill scores to evaluate how well you have mastered this step.

This final step is all about playing as a team. Cricket requires individuals to perform for themselves but at the same time contribute to the team. A batsman might score a century, but his side loses. A bowler might not take a wicket, but his team triumphs. This is why it is so important that every cricketer is a team player. A team player does not blame others for failings or take all the praise for a success. He knows that however grand or minimal his contribution, it is the team's result that counts. There is no better feeling than to be part of a successful team, and that takes precedence over individual glory, for that on its own rarely ensures team success. There are many examples of teams made up of 11 ordinary cricketers playing to potential and defeating a team that relies on one or two outstanding individuals. Adopt this team ethic and you will get true enjoyment and fulfilment from this best of all sports—cricket.

Team Roles Drills

   1. Hit to the Marked Zone   ___ out of 5

   2. Quick Running   ___ out of 5

Total   ___ *out of 10*

Glossary

all-rounder—Player who specialises in more than one discipline; usually a batsman and bowler, but the term can apply to a batsman and a wicket-keeper.

appeal—When the umpire is asked to adjudicate on a dismissal by the bowler or fielders. "How's that?" or "How is he?" are the usual appeals, truncated to "howzat" or "howzee."

away-swing—A ball that moves through the air from leg to off as it approaches the batsman; also known as an out-swing.

back-foot drive—An attacking shot from a batsman who has moved backwards before hitting the ball back past the bowler.

backward defensive—A defensive shot from a batsman who moves backwards in his crease and then blocks the ball from hitting his wicket.

backward point—Single-saver fielding position whose primary function is to prevent batsmen from taking quick runs or force batsmen to run them out if they try; will try to stop the fours and will accept any catches that come his way.

ball—Refers either to the spherical object that is bowled and hit or to a delivery ("That was a good ball").

bouncer—A short ball from a quick bowler that rears up towards the batsman's head or upper body.

bowler—The player who bowls the ball.

bowling crease—Location of the stumps and from where the bowler must deliver the ball.

captain—The player who is in charge of the team on the field.

cover point—Single-saver fielding position whose primary function is to prevent batsmen from taking quick runs or force batsmen to run them out if they try; will try to stop the fours and will accept any catches that come his way.

crease—The markings of the pitch, explained in figure 3 on page xiv.

cutter—A ball the bowler makes cut off the pitch to deceive the batsman by deviation on bouncing.

deep mid-wicket—Deep fielder position whose primary role is to prevent the ball from crossing the boundary for four.

deep point—Deep fielder position whose primary role is to prevent the ball from crossing the boundary for four.

deep square leg—Deep fielder position whose primary role is to prevent the ball from crossing the boundary for four.

extra cover—Single-saver fielding position whose primary function is to prevent batsmen from taking quick runs or force batsmen to run them out if they try; will try to stop the fours and will accept any catches that come his way.

fine leg—Deep fielder position whose primary role is to prevent the ball from crossing the boundary for four.

forward defensive—A defensive stroke from a batsman who moves forward to prevent the ball from hitting the wicket.

front-foot drive—An attacking stroke played when the batsman moves forward to strike the ball back past the bowler.

googly—A ball delivered with an action that makes it appear as a leg break, but it turns the other way.

gully—Close-catcher fielding position in which the fielder accepts any chance of a catch; used when the batting team is on the attack and taking wickets is the primary goal.

hook—An exciting shot played by a batsman to a short ball that is rising towards him.

in-swing—A ball that moves from off to leg through the air as it approaches the batsman.

leg before wicket (LBW)—A means by which the bowler dismisses the batsman when the pad gets in the way of the wicket.

leg glance—Can be played off the back or front foot; involves diverting the ball down the leg side.

long barrier—A fielding technique that involves going down on one knee and presenting a barrier between the ball and the boundary.

long leg—Deep fielder position whose primary role is to prevent the ball from crossing the boundary for four.

long-off—Deep fielder position whose primary role is to prevent the ball from crossing the boundary for four.

long-on—Deep fielder position whose primary role is to prevent the ball from crossing the boundary for four.

maiden—An over off which no runs (other than byes or leg byes) are scored.

mid-off—Single-saver fielding position whose primary function is to prevent batsmen from taking quick runs or force batsmen to run them out if they try; will try to stop the fours and will accept any catches that come his way.

mid-on—Single-saver fielding position whose primary function is to prevent batsmen from taking quick runs or force batsmen to run them out if they try; will try to stop the fours and will accept any catches that come his way.

mid-wicket—Single-saver fielding position whose primary function is to prevent batsmen from taking quick runs or force batsmen to run them out if they try; will try to stop the fours and will accept any catches that come his way.

no-ball—When a bowler transgresses the Laws as he delivers the ball.

non-striker—The batsman in the middle who is not facing the bowling.

off side—The side of the pitch to the right of a batsman turned front on to the bowler.

on side—The side of the pitch to the left of a batsman turned front on to the bowler.

one-day cricket—Matches played over a set number of overs rather than over time.

pace bowler—A bowler who relies primarily on speed to dismiss the batsman.

pitch—The 22 yards between the two wickets and the immediate surrounding area. The pitch of the ball is where the ball lands after it has been bowled.

point—Single-saver fielding position whose primary function is to prevent batsmen from taking quick runs or force batsmen to run them out if they try; will try to stop the fours and will accept any catches that come his way.

popping crease—The area in which the batsman must stay to avoid being stumped or run out.

pull—A shot played to the leg side against a short ball.

return crease—The line running perpendicular to the popping crease behind which the bowler must ground his back foot at the moment he delivers the ball.

reverse cup—The position a fielder uses when he turns his palms towards the ball and his fingers point upwards or back towards his face.

run-out—A means of dismissing the batsman when he has not reached his crease by the time the ball hits the wicket at the end to which he is running, or when a fielder catches the ball and removes the bails before the batsman gets in.

short leg—Close-catcher fielding position in which the fielder accepts any chance of a catch; used when the batting team is on the attack and taking wickets is the primary goal.

silly mid-off—Close-catcher fielding position in which the fielder accepts any chance of a catch; used when the batting team is on the attack and taking wickets is the primary goal.

silly mid-on—Close-catcher fielding position in which the fielder accepts any chance of a catch; used when the batting team is on the attack and taking wickets is the primary goal.

silly point—Close-catcher fielding position in which the fielder accepts any chance of a catch; used when the batting team is on the attack and taking wickets is the primary goal.

slip—Close-catcher fielding position in which the fielder accepts any chance of a catch; used when the batting team is on the attack and taking wickets is the primary goal.

slip cordon—The line of slip fielders waiting for a catch.

slog-sweep—A shot played by a batsman when he plays a sweep in the air rather than along the ground.

spinner—A bowler who imparts spin on the ball so it deviates off the pitch on bouncing.

square leg—Single-saver fielding position whose primary function is to prevent batsmen from taking quick runs or force batsmen to run them out if they try; will try to stop the fours and will accept any catches that come his way.

standing back—The position a wicket-keeper takes some way behind the wicket as he prepares to take the ball from a quicker bowler.

standing up—The position a wicket-keeper takes within arm's reach of the wicket as he prepares to take the ball from a slower bowler.

striker—The batsman who is facing the bowler.

stumping—When a wicket-keeper takes the ball and removes the bails with the batsman out of his crease.

sweep—A shot to leg played by a batsman going down on one knee.

Test match—A match played over five days between top international teams.

tail—lower-order batsmen.

third man—Deep fielder position whose primary role is to prevent the ball from crossing the boundary for four.

Twenty20—The shortest form of the game played at the top level, in which each side has only 20 overs to bat.

wicket—The three stumps and two bails that constitute the target at which a bowler aims. It also refers to a batsman being out. Sometimes, erroneously, it is a term used instead of pitch.

wicket-keeper—The fielder with pads and gloves who stands immediately behind the wicket, waiting to take the ball should the batsman miss it, and the ball miss the stumps.

wide—A ball that is bowled too wide of the stumps for a batsman to be able to hit. This adds a run to the total, and another ball has to be bowled that over.

yorker—A ball of full length that lands on the popping crease and goes under the bat.

About the Author

Ralph Dellor has been involved with cricket for over 50 years as a player, broadcaster, journalist and coach. In a career that has taken him to some 25 countries, he has coached the England women's team and was on the coaching staff at Oxford University. More recently, Ralph has been coach of the Norwegian national team that has risen from relative obscurity to enter the first division of European cricket.

Fully involved in spreading cricket's popularity, Dellor was the first chairman of the England and Wales Cricket Board Coaches Association, worked for the International Cricket Council, was a selector for the England Amateur XI, serves on the Berkshire County Cricket Club committee and is chairman of his local village club. He was also a member of the UK Sports Council and an advisor to a former UK minister for sport.

STEPS TO SUCCESS SPORTS SERIES

The *Steps to Success Sports Series* is the most extensively researched and carefully developed set of books ever published for teaching and learning sports skills.

Each of the books offers a complete progression of skills, concepts and strategies that are carefully sequenced to optimize learning for students, teaching for sport-specific instructors and instructional program design techniques for future teachers.

The *Steps to Success Sports Series* includes:

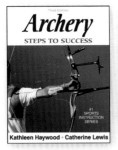

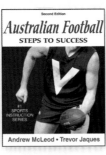

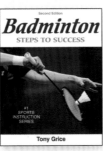

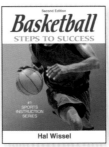

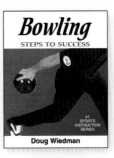

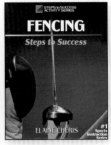

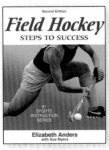

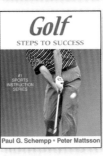

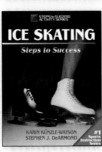

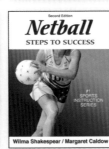

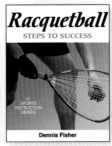

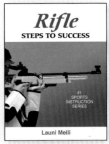

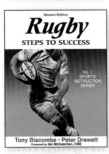

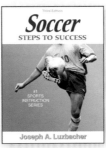

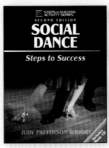

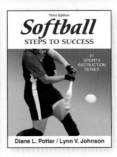

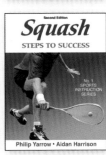

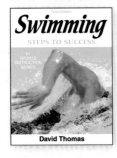

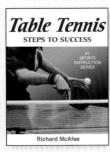

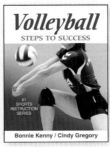

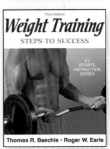

To place your order, U.S. customers call
TOLL FREE **1-800-747-4457**
In Canada call 1-800-465-7301
In Australia call 08 8372 0999
In Europe call +44 (0) 113 255 5665
In New Zealand call 0800 222 062
or visit **www.HumanKinetics.com**

HUMAN KINETICS
The Premier Publisher for Sports & Fitness
P.O. Box 5076, Champaign, IL 61825-5076